中国环境

资源审判

（2021）

中华人民共和国最高人民法院 编

人民法院出版社

图书在版编目（CIP）数据
中国环境资源审判. 2021 : 汉文、英文 / 中华人民共和国最高人民法院编. -- 北京 : 人民法院出版社, 2024. 12. -- ISBN 978-7-5109-4320-1
Ⅰ. D922.684
中国国家版本馆CIP数据核字第2024U86Q04号

中国环境资源审判（2021）

中华人民共和国最高人民法院　编

责任编辑　巩　雪
执行编辑　沈洁雯
出版发行　人民法院出版社
地　　址　北京市东城区东交民巷 27 号（100745）
电　　话　（010）67550667（执行编辑）　67550558（发行部查询）
　　　　　65223677（读者服务部）
客服 QQ　2092078039
网　　址　http://www.courtbook.com.cn
E - mail　courtpress@sohu.com
印　　刷　北京瑞禾彩色印刷有限公司
经　　销　新华书店

开　　本　787×1092 毫米　1/16
字　　数　84 千字
印　　张　5.5
版　　次　2024 年 12 月第 1 版　2024 年 12 月第 1 次印刷
书　　号　ISBN 978-7-5109-4320-1
定　　价　28.00 元

中国环境资源审判（2021）

Environment and Resources Adjudication in China（2021）

编辑委员会

Editorial Committee Members

目　　录

Contents

引　言

2021年是人民法院环境资源审判发展史上具有里程碑意义的一年。5月26日，习近平主席向世界环境司法大会致贺信指出："地球是我们的共同家园。世界各国要同心协力，抓紧行动，共建人和自然和谐的美丽家园。中国坚持创新、协调、绿色、开放、共享的新发展理念，全面加强生态环境保护工作，积极参与全球生态文明建设合作。中国持续深化环境司法改革创新，积累了生态环境司法保护的有益经验。中国愿同世界各国、国际组织携手合作，共同推进全球生态环境治理。"① 习近平主席的贺信充分肯定了中国环境司法改革创新的有益经验，为人民法院环境资源审判指明了发展方向，提供了根本遵循。12月10日，最高人民法院召开第三次全国环境资源审判工作会议，系统总结三年来的工作，分析环境资源审判面临的形势任务，从服务保障美丽中国建设大局、着力构建中国特色环境资源审判体系、积极推动生态环境法律适用规则体系化、努力打造高素质专业化环境资源审判队伍等方面作出具体工作部署，明确了推进工作的总体思路和发展方向，开启了环境资源审判工作新征程。

2021年，全国法院坚持以习近平新时代中国特色社会主义思想为指导，深入贯彻习近平生态文明思想和习近平法治思想，认真落实习近平主席致世界环境司法大会贺信重要指示，紧紧围绕统筹推进"五位一体"总体布局和协调推进"四个全面"战略布局，牢牢把握以人民为中心的发展思想，立足新发展阶段，完整准确全面贯彻新发展理念，构建新发展格局，促进高质量发展，坚持以构建中国特色环境

① 《习近平向世界环境司法大会致贺信》，载《人民日报》2021年5月27日，第1版。

资源审判体系为主线，以推进审判专业化建设为抓手，以深化改革创新为动力，以提升智慧司法水平为支撑，以拓展国际合作交流为平台，充分发挥环境资源审判职能作用，各项工作迈上新台阶。

依法公正审理各类案件。2021 年，全国法院共受理环境资源一审案件 297 492 件，审结 265 341 件，同比分别上升 8. 99%、4. 76%。加大对污染环境、破坏生态犯罪行为的惩治力度，维护国家生态环境和自然资源安全，受理环境资源刑事一审案件 39 023 件，审结 35 460 件。依法追究污染环境、破坏生态行为人的民事责任，受理环境资源民事一审案件 185 468 件，审结 167 055 件。充分发挥行政审判预防和监督功能，支持、监督行政机关依法及时履行监管职责，受理环境资源行政一审案件 73 001 件，审结 62 826 件。加强环境公益诉讼和生态环境损害赔偿诉讼案件审理，切实维护国家利益、社会公共利益和人民群众环境权益，受理环境公益诉讼案件 5917 件，审结 4943 件；受理生态环境损害赔偿案件 169 件，审结 137 件。

服务保障新时代美丽中国建设大局，助力深入打好污染防治攻坚战，落实生物多样性保护国家战略，促进资源高效节约合理利用，服务绿色低碳循环发展，助力产业结构优化升级，服务国家区域发展战略，推动重点流域区域系统治理。坚持良法善治，出台新时代加强和创新环境资源审判工作的意见，制定适用禁止令、惩罚性赔偿等司法解释和会议纪要，发布指导性案例和典型案例，创新审判执行方式，拓展延伸审判职能，不断完善生态环境裁判规则体系。坚持创新引领，加强环境资源专门审判机构建设，完善归口审理、集中管辖、司法协作、协调联动和多元解纷机制，专门化环境资源审判体系基本建成。加强审判队伍思想政治和专业化建设，深化审判理论研究，完善司法便民利民惠民举措，推进司法公开，深化公众参与，不断提升环境资源司法服务保障水平。深化国际交流，成功举办世界环境司法大会，起草并推动通过《世界环境司法大会昆明宣言》，在联合国环境规划署网站刊登中国环境资源典型案例和白皮书，分享交流中国环境司法的有益经验。

一、充分发挥审判职能作用，服务保障新时代美丽中国建设大局

（一）助力深入打好污染防治攻坚战，依法审理环境污染防治案件

贯彻落实《中共中央、国务院关于深入打好污染防治攻坚战的意见》，坚持良好生态环境是最普惠的民生福祉，充分运用司法手段切实维护人民群众环境权益。各级人民法院依法严厉打击暗管偷排、跨域倾倒、非法处置污染物等突出违法犯罪行为，审理涉大气、水、土壤、固体废物及噪声污染等案件，推动解决人民群众身边突出的环境污染问题。依法审理涉城市重污染天气、黑臭水体整治、医疗废物处置等案件，持续改善城市人居环境。依法审理涉农业面源污染、农用地土壤污染、生活垃圾分类等案件，服务美丽乡村建设。

最高人民法院发布涉及大气、水、土壤、固体废物、噪声污染典型案例，深化污染防治司法指引。积极参与《噪声污染防治法》修改论证，提出法律责任相关条文修改建议，为《噪声污染防治法》修改工作提供司法实践支持。京津冀、长江、黄河流域等地法院加大对辖区突出环境问题的司法治理，以更高标准打好蓝天、碧水、净土保卫战。各地法院加强医疗废物处置相关案件审理，司法助力疫情防控，维护公共卫生安全。上海法院审理涉“洋垃圾”环境民事公益诉讼案，强化固体废物污染责任追究，改善人居环境。

2021 年，全国法院受理污染环境犯罪案件 2837 件，审结 2328 件；受理走私废物犯罪案件 198 件，审结 167 件；受理涉大气、水、土壤、

固体废物、噪声污染等环境污染纠纷案件 1817 件，审结 1361 件；受理海上、通海水域污染损害责任纠纷案件 26 件，审结 20 件；受理船舶污染损害责任纠纷案件 17 件，审结 9 件；受理环保行政案件 3377 件，审结 2743 件。

（二）落实生物多样性保护国家战略，依法审理生态保护案件

贯彻落实中共中央办公厅、国务院办公厅《关于进一步加强生物多样性保护的意见》，系统保护珍贵、濒危野生动植物及其生存环境，维护生物多样性和生物安全。各级人民法院依法审理涉遗传多样性、物种多样性和生态系统多样性保护案件，严厉打击各类破坏野生动植物资源犯罪活动，依法惩治利用网络或以其他方式实施野生动植物及制品非法贸易，非法引进、释放或丢弃外来物种等违法犯罪行为。加大对国家公园、自然保护区等各类自然公园的司法保护力度，保护珍贵濒危野生动植物栖息地生态环境，护航候鸟安全迁徙。统筹疫情防控与生物多样性司法保护，助推国家生物安全治理能力水平不断提升。

最高人民法院发布“绿孔雀保护”预防性公益诉讼案等首批 7 个生物多样性保护专题指导性案例，明确生物种群及其生存环境司法保护的裁判规则。长江流域相关法院严格落实《长江保护法》，通过发布司法保护意见、加强区域司法协作、对非法捕捞犯罪实施全链条打击等方式，促进长江水生生物资源恢复，服务长江十年禁渔。重庆法院审理黎某建等非法捕捞水产品犯罪案，在惩处被告人的同时，依法规制被告人自行投放对当地生态环境有害的外来物种的行为，明确增殖放流应当采取符合生态环境特点的方式，维护当地生物多样性和水域生态安全。

2021 年，全国法院受理走私珍贵动物、珍贵动物制品犯罪案件 155 件，审结 113 件；受理危害珍贵、濒危野生动物犯罪案件 3262 件，审结 2944 件；受理非法猎捕、收购、运输、出售陆生野生动物犯罪案件 177 件，审结 154 件；受理非法狩猎犯罪案件 3694 件，审结 3549 件；

受理非法捕捞水产品犯罪案件 5950 件，审结 5714 件；受理危害国家重点保护植物犯罪案件 875 件，审结 839 件；受理盗伐林木犯罪案件 1481 件，审结 1407 件；受理滥伐林木犯罪案件 5663 件，审结 5334 件；受理动植物检疫徇私舞弊犯罪案件 18 件，审结 13 件；受理林业行政案件 4251 件，审结 3697 件；受理渔业行政案件 303 件，审结 281 件。

（三）促进资源高效节约合理利用，依法审理资源开发利用案件

贯彻落实“绿水青山就是金山银山”的理念，正确处理人与自然、保护与发展的关系，全面提高资源利用效率。各级人民法院依法惩治非法采矿采砂、非法侵占河湖、乱砍滥伐、毁林挖草、非法开垦等破坏生态的违法犯罪活动。依法审理涉土地、草原、矿藏、森林、海域等自然资源权属案件，科学划定自然资源所有权、使用权行使边界，维护全民所有自然资源资产所有者权益。完善自然资源权属争议行政调处与司法审判的衔接，服务构建市场化、多元化的生态保护补偿机制。

最高人民法院起草关于严惩盗采矿产资源犯罪的意见，立足服务经济社会高质量发展，正确认识和把握严惩犯罪、保护生态与发展经济、保障民生之间的辩证关系，充分发挥环境资源审判职能作用，依法严惩盗采矿产资源犯罪，有效整治和防范盗采矿产资源行为，维护矿产资源和生态环境安全。黑龙江法院审理王某等非法采矿犯罪案，对王某等人非法开采泥炭土犯罪行为予以严厉打击，司法保护黑土地这一“耕地中的大熊猫”。

2021 年，全国法院受理非法采矿犯罪案件 4245 件，审结 3549 件；受理非法收购、运输盗伐、滥伐的林木犯罪案件 162 件，审结 158 件；受理非法占用农用地犯罪案件 3594 件，审结 3489 件；受理建设用地使用权纠纷案件 5158 件，审结 3932 件；受理地役权纠纷案件 83 件，审结 75 件；受理海洋开发利用纠纷案件 69 件，审结 55 件；受理取水权纠纷案件 26 件，审结 25 件；受理矿业权纠纷案件 548 件，审结 423

件；受理供用电、水、气、热力合同纠纷案件 58 647 件，审结 55 517 件；受理中外合作勘探开发自然资源合同纠纷案件 3 件，审结 3 件；受理农业、林业、渔业、牧业承包合同纠纷案件 11 202 件，审结 9874 件；受理土地行政案件 35 988 件，审结 31 418 件；受理地矿行政案件 700 件，审结 609 件；受理水利行政案件 847 件，审结 699 件；受理其他资源行政案件 17 785 件，审结 15 371 件。

（四）服务绿色低碳循环发展，依法审理气候变化应对案件

贯彻落实《中共中央、国务院关于完整准确全面贯彻新发展理念做好碳达峰碳中和工作的意见》，推动减污降碳协同增效，助力实现碳达峰碳中和目标。各级人民法院依法审理碳排放重点行业领域及新能源开发利用的节能减排案件，在能源、交通、臭氧层物质消耗、土地和林业利用等领域减少或避免温室气体排放，应对全球气候变化危机。准确把握碳排放权、碳汇、碳衍生品等涉碳权利的经济属性、公共属性和生态属性，依法妥当处理涉及确权、交易、担保以及执行的相关涉碳民事纠纷。监督和支持行政机关依法查处碳排放单位虚报、瞒报温室气体排放数据、拒绝履行温室气体排放报告义务等违法行为。

最高人民法院专题研究碳排放权交易纠纷司法规则，起草司法助力实现碳达峰碳中和目标的指导意见、审理涉森林资源民事案件司法解释。各地法院严格执行国家减污降碳相关法律法规政策要求，积极探索新型涉碳纠纷特点，依法审理涉碳案件，共助碳达峰碳中和目标实现。江苏、上海、浙江、福建四地海事法院签订保护东海海洋资源与生态环境框架协议，保护海洋“蓝碳”资源；四川法院建立“绿色金融诉源治理工作站”，密切跟进碳排放权、用能权等环境权益交易及融资纠纷法律适用等问题；广东法院妥善审理涉碳排放权交易合同纠纷案件，厘清交易各方的责任承担；浙江、湖北等高院发布工作意见，服务保障碳达峰碳中和。

（五）助力产业结构优化升级，依法审理生态环境治理与服务案件

贯彻落实生态优先、绿色发展原则，司法服务供给侧结构性改革，促进经济社会发展全面绿色转型。各级人民法院依法审理涉及环境影响评价、环境监测、环境损害评估鉴定、生态环境监测设备及污染防治设施维护运营、生态环境修复等方面案件。妥善审理涉高耗能、高排放企业规划、建设、生产纠纷，鼓励清洁生产，推动重点行业和重要领域绿色化改造。加大对高耗能、高排放企业改制、破产和重整案件审理力度，完善市场退出机制。支持运用金融工具助力绿色发展，支持保险机构创新绿色保险产品和服务，促进绿色金融市场健康发展。

各地法院在民事诉讼法行为保全制度框架之下，积极探索禁止令在环境污染和生态破坏案件中的适用，及时防止或减少生态环境损害，强化生态环境风险预防。福建法院创新“生态司法+救助保险”，与保险公司签订合作协议，将被告人、侵权人缴纳的生态修复资金转入保险公司专门账户，江西法院探索委托公益性基金会管理和监督使用生态环境修复资金并组织实施环境修复，有效规范修复资金的管理和使用。浙江法院审理高耗能、高排放企业破产清算转重整案，设置“环保承诺”投资条件，推动企业通过重整重获新生并走上绿色低碳转型的全新发展道路。

（六）服务国家区域协调发展，推动重点流域区域系统治理

贯彻落实共同抓好大保护、协同推进大治理原则，主动将生态司法保护融入长江经济带发展、粤港澳大湾区建设、长三角一体化发展、黄河流域生态保护和高质量发展等区域重大发展战略实施。各级人民法院依法审理涉长江黄河干流和重要支流环境污染案件，审理大运河、长城等文化公园保护案件，审理涉传统民居、古村落、古建筑保护等

案件，维护人民群众环境权益。贯彻冰天雪地也是金山银山理念，依法审理涉青藏高原生态环境保护案件，切实保护好地球第三极生态。妥善审理涉京津风沙源治理、三江源生态保护和建设、祁连山生态保护与综合治理、岩溶地区石漠化综合治理等国家重点生态功能区修复保护相关案件，加大对水土流失、土地沙化、石漠化、海岸侵蚀及沙源流失等生态极度脆弱区生态环境的司法保护力度，维护国家生态安全。

最高人民法院出台有关贯彻《长江保护法》实施意见，召开贯彻实施《长江保护法》工作推进会和黄河、大运河、南水北调工程流域环境资源审判工作推进会，发布相关会议纪要和典型案例，为各级法院服务国家区域发展战略、推动大江大河等重点区域流域系统治理提供裁判规则指引。各地法院深化重点区域环境资源案件集中管辖与司法协作。安徽、江西、湖北、湖南法院签署长江中下游环资司法协作机制合作协议，就加强长江中下游跨区域环境司法协作达成共识；河北组织大运河沿线 8 家基层法院签署大运河（沧州段）司法协作协议，实行一体化保护。北京法院审理“长城保护案”，加强历史文化遗产保护。

二、坚持良法善治，不断完善环境资源审判规则体系

（一）深化司法政策顶层设计

最高人民法院召开第三次全国法院环境资源审判工作会议，系统总结工作成效，深入分析形势任务，提出构建有中国特色和国际影响力审判体系的工作主线，明确为建设人与自然和谐共生的现代化，协

同推进人民富裕、国家强盛、中国美丽提供有力司法服务和保障的工作总目标，并从服务美丽中国建设大局、深化改革创新、推动法律适用规则体系化、建设高素质专业化审判队伍、深化国际交流合作等方面，对推进环境资源审判工作进行了科学谋划和具体部署。出台《最高人民法院关于新时代加强和创新环境资源审判工作为建设人与自然和谐共生的现代化提供司法服务和保障的意见》，对新时代人民法院环境资源审判工作各领域、各环节提出全方位的指导意见和具体要求。出台《环境资源案件类型与统计规范（试行）》，指导各级法院合理划定环境资源案件范围和环境资源审判机构的职责范围，确保环境资源审判聚焦主责主业。黑龙江、吉林、贵州、青海等高院结合辖区特点出台规范性意见，推动环境资源审判工作高质量发展。

（二）完善法律适用规则

最高人民法院出台《最高人民法院关于生态环境侵权案件适用禁止令保全措施的若干规定》，落实保护优先、预防为主原则，及时有效保护生态环境，维护民事主体合法权益。出台《最高人民法院关于审理生态环境侵权纠纷案件适用惩罚性赔偿的解释》，贯彻落实用最严格制度最严密法治保护生态环境，加大对恶意损害生态环境行为司法惩治力度，找准环境司法审判统筹生态环境保护、经济社会发展和保障民生的平衡点。此两部司法解释的制定和出台，为生态环境保护起到了跨越式的作用，也受到各级法院的普遍欢迎，得到相关行政部门和学界的充分肯定。起草涉森林资源民事纠纷、环境侵权民事诉讼证据规则、具有专门知识的人员作为人民陪审员参与环境资源案件审理等司法解释，不断完善审判规则体系。海南、重庆高院出台量刑指引，贵州高院出台审理指南，山东、河南高院出台案由规定等文件，进一步加强环境资源案件审理。

（三）发挥案例示范引领和规则补充作用

最高人民法院加强环境资源案例指导，健全指导性案例的发现、培育和推荐工作机制，提高编选案例的针对性、科学性和操作性，明确法律适用标准。2021年发布首批7件生物多样性保护专题指导性案例，并已启动第二批环境公益诉讼专题指导性案例的遴选工作。充分发挥典型案例示范引领作用，加强疑难复杂新类型案件法律适用问题研究，促进环境资源领域类型化案件裁判尺度统一。2021年发布长江、黄河生态环境保护典型案例及2020年度典型案例共30个，调解结案中华环保联合会诉国能辽宁某产业集团有限公司等环境污染民事公益诉讼再审案，促进生态环境及时有效修复。根据四级法院审级职能定位改革要求，不断完善环境资源案件提级管辖机制，对新类型、具有普遍法律适用指导意义、存在重大法律适用分歧的案件提级管辖，弥补裁判规则供给不足的问题。四川法院审理五小叶槭保护公益诉讼案，对加强珍贵、濒危野生植物预防性司法保护具有指导意义。江西法院审理非法倾倒化工废液环境污染公益诉讼案，对正确适用《民法典》生态环境侵权惩罚性赔偿条款作出有益探索。

（四）创新审判执行方式，拓展延伸审判职能

坚持恢复性司法，立足不同环境要素的修复需求，创新适用多种符合生态环境保护要求的修复方式。山东法院审理汽车制造公司大气污染民事公益诉讼案，探索“绿色执行”，促使被告企业以捐献新能源电动汽车用于公益事业的方式实现生态修复，统筹协调经济发展与环境保护。江西法院探索通过公益信托方式委托生态环境基金会监管公益诉讼修复资金，并组织生态环境修复，取得良好效果。福建、浙江、四川、贵州法院在案件审理或执行中，以侵权人认购碳汇的方式履行生态环境修复责任，推动减污降碳。新疆、宁夏法院建立执行回访机制，确保生态环境修复义务得到有效履行。

贯彻恢复性司法要求，探索创新裁判方式。在刑事案件中，将被告人具有积极修复生态环境，开展符合自然规律的植树造林、增殖放流等情形，作为从轻量刑情节予以考虑，促进受损生态环境及时修复。在民事案件中，将当事企业在已符合国家环境标准情况下继续实行技术升级改造的资金，以技改抵扣的方式折抵生态环境修复费用，推动企业绿色转型升级。充分发挥生态环境修复基地作用，开展多元化的生态保护、宣传、修复等工作。湖北法院在重点区域设立 44 个保护基地；甘肃法院发挥修复基地作用，累计复绿面积 8600 亩，补种补植逾 15 万余株，年均中和二氧化碳量约 9886 吨。

三、坚持创新引领，着力构建中国特色环境资源审判体系

（一）环境资源审判组织体系基本形成

截至 2021 年年底，全国共设立环境资源专门审判机构和审判组织 2149 个，其中环境资源审判庭 649 个（包括最高人民法院、29 家高级人民法院、新疆生产建设兵团分院、158 家中级人民法院及 460 家基层人民法院），人民法庭 215 个，审判团队（合议庭）1285 个。继设立南京、兰州环境资源法庭之后，最高人民法院批准设立昆明、郑州环境资源法庭，探索专门审判机构新实践。各地法院在重点流域、世界自然遗产、江河源头、国家公园、自然保护区等设立巡回法庭、环保法庭、旅游法庭等，加强重点生态功能区司法保护。山东全省 16 个地级市全部成立环境资源审判庭，155 个基层法院明确 187 个环境资源审判机构；贵州设立传统村落司法保护法官工作站 114 个。

（二）案件归口审理和集中管辖机制广泛推行

2021年，最高人民法院实现环境资源刑事、民事、行政审判职能归口至环境资源审判庭行使，进一步完善对下监督指导。全国共有27家高级人民法院及新疆生产建设兵团分院实行环境资源刑事、民事、行政案件“三合一”归口审理模式，其中江西、云南等高院实行刑事、民事、行政、执行案件的“四合一”归口审理执行模式。

完善多元化跨行政区划集中管辖模式。昆明环境资源法庭集中管辖云南全省原由中级人民法院受理的环境资源一审、二审和再审案件。郑州环境资源法庭集中管辖淮河干流、南水北调工程沿线环境资源案件。湖北法院初步形成由高院、中院、生态环境保护法庭和审判团队组成的“1+5+10+N”环资审判专门化体系。海南高院与检察机关、海警局联合会签特定海事刑事案件集中指定管辖试点工作意见，集中指定海事法院管辖海上交通肇事罪和破坏海洋生态环境资源犯罪两类案件。浙江将湖州地区环资案件管辖模式调整为“南太湖法院全域集中管辖+安吉等重点区域指定管辖”。四川设立大熊猫国家公园生态法庭，负责集中管辖大熊猫国家公园四川片区范围内的相关案件，实现区域环境资源一体化司法保护。

（三）司法协作机制建设更加成熟

各地法院落实一体化保护和系统治理原则，结合重点区域流域特点，不断深化环境资源司法协作。最高人民法院召开黄河、大运河、南水北调工程流域环境资源审判工作推进会，进一步加强黄河、大运河及南水北调工程流域内生态环境及文化资源司法保护和协作。河南、湖北、陕西高院签署环丹江口水库生态环境保护与修复协作协议；黑龙江与内蒙古高院会签东北边疆两省（区）林草、湿地、野生动物资源保护环境资源审判协作协议；河南与北京两地法院立足南水北调中线工程首尾区域，签订共建法治保水司法示范基地合作协议；湖北、湖南、江西高院签署构建长江中游城市群审判工作协作机制；天津、辽宁、山东签署渤海生态环境保护司法协作协议；浙江东海沿岸七家中院及海事法院建立“1+7”环东海司法协作机制，不断加强重点区域流域司法协作。

（四）跨部门联动机制建设不断拓展

最高人民法院与推动黄河流域生态保护和高质量发展领导小组办公室签署协同治理合作协议，与生态环境部座谈，推进行政执法与司法的协调联动。各地法院联合生态环境部门等单位出台生态环境和资源保护行政执法与司法协作机制的意见，破解区域司法行政保护衔接难题。江苏、上海、浙江法院与生态环境部门等共同签署长三角一体化示范区生态环境检查执法互认机制对接会议纪要；广西高院与行政部门会签漓江流域、北部湾海洋生态环境保护合作框架协议；陕西高院与检察机关等部门会签涉林业行政执法与刑事司法衔接办法；辽宁、天津等地法院与检察机关就环境公益诉讼等案件的审理会签意见；海南高院与检察机关联合出台量刑指导意见，对热带雨林国家公园常见的盗伐林木和滥伐林木两类案件量刑进行规范，助力海南热带雨林国家公园建设。

（五）多元解纷机制建设有效运转

各地法院推动运用调解、协商、仲裁等多元化纠纷解决方式，更加高效便捷地满足人民群众多元化环境司法需求。充分发挥司法建议积极作用，广东法院在办理涉野生动物刑事案件过程中，提出司法建议协调某互联网公司删除违规网帖3万余条，对175组涉野生动物关键词进行拦截，并向公安机关提供犯罪线索。发扬新时代“枫桥经验”，发挥人民法庭、巡回审判参与基层环境治理作用，打造基层环境司法化解矛盾的样本。云南普洱思茅区人民法院主动延伸司法职能，在“亚洲象繁育中心”驻地挂牌成立全国首家“人象和谐法律服务点”，加强人象矛盾纠纷源头预防和前端化解，推动人象矛盾纠纷化解进入法治绿色通道，探索诉源治理与环境资源审判新模式。福建法院探索林长制与司法的融合，立足涉林生态治理的重点领域，建立涉林生态纠纷诉前化解网格。

四、加强队伍建设，努力提升环境资源司法服务水平

（一）深化理论研究，提升专业能力

深化司法实践与理论交流互动。发挥最高人民法院环境司法研究中心作用，开展《民法典》绿色条款法律适用等实践问题研究工作，举办《民法典》绿色原则征文评选暨专题研讨，推动理论与实践融合发展。各理论基地和实践基地在2021年发布各类研究成果24项。2021年，最高人民法院上线全国法院环境资源审判线上培训课程；与中华环保基金会合作举办中西部环境资源法官培训班；创办“绿色发展论坛”，邀请国内外专家学者、资深法官开展业务交流，赴浙江、陕西、云南等地开展环境资源审判集中调研；开展全国环境资源审判优秀裁判文书、优秀业务成果评选，云南、重庆、江苏等法院15篇裁判文书，北京、浙江、广东等法院19项调研成果获奖，有力提升队伍专业能力。各地法院根据环境资源审判专门化要求，加强培训，开展专题调研，提升审判队伍业务能力。

（二）畅通诉讼渠道，完善便民措施

最高人民法院全面推行一站式多元纠纷解决和诉讼服务，健全司

法便民利民惠民举措，持续增加优质环境司法服务供给。积极推进智慧法院建设，加快建设中国环境资源司法平台。通过网上立案、跨域立案、在线开庭，巡回审判，方便当事人参加诉讼。重庆法院设立环境资源司法协作巡回法庭，为川渝两地群众提供高效便捷的立审执一体化跨域诉讼服务；江苏法院设立“古城大运河司法保护巡回审判站”，开展社区巡回审判；新疆法院采取“定点+流动”的巡回审判模式，进驻巡回审判点提供“上门式”司法服务；山东法院在微山湖流域使用审判船开展巡回审判，将司法服务延伸到群众身边。

（三）推进司法公开，深化公众参与

各级人民法院严格落实公开审判制度，通过中国庭审公开网、微信公众号、微博等多种传播媒介同步直播案件庭审，对辖区内有重大影响的环境资源案件，主动邀请人大代表、政协委员以及相关企业和公众代表、学生等到庭旁听，提升审判的公开性、透明度。2021 年最高人民法院召开 6 次涉环境资源审判的新闻发布会，发布司法解释、指导性案例等；邀请 85 名全国人大代表、全国政协委员线上参加第三次全国环境资源审判工作会议等重要活动。通过“中国环境资源审判”微信公众号加强环境司法宣传。指导各级人民法院在“六·五环境日”等重要时间节点组织新闻发布会发布年度报告、典型案例及公开审理案件等形式多样的宣传活动，形成集约示范效应，有效扩大环境司法影响力。对于涉及环境民事公益诉讼案件、生态环境损害赔偿诉讼案件的起诉、调解协议、修复方案等，严格落实公告程序，接受公众监督，保障人民群众对环境司法的知情权、参与权和监督权。

五、深化国际交流，分享交流中国环境司法有益经验

（一）成功举办世界环境司法大会

2021 年 5 月，最高人民法院与联合国环境规划署共同成功举办作为《生物多样性公约》第十五次缔约方大会的，以“发挥司法作用促进生态文明：共建地球生命共同体”为主题的世界环境司法大会。习近平主席向大会致贺信，充分肯定中国环境司法改革创新有益经验，为加强环境司法国际交流合作、促进世界环境法治指明了方向。时任最高人民法院院长周强发表主旨演讲，全面展现中国生态环境司法保护的生动实践。来自俄罗斯、法国等 27 个国家最高法院、宪法法院、最高行政法院的院长或法官，联合国环境规划署等国际组织代表和驻华使节，以及最高人民法院、云南等 8 家高院院长等中外代表共计 160 余人参加会议。与会代表围绕司法在全球环境治理中的作用、环境司法的裁判原则、生物多样性司法保护、气候变化司法应对等议题开展了深入交流探讨，一致通过《世界环境司法大会昆明宣言》。世界环境司法大会的成功举办，凝聚了全球生态环境司法保护国际共识，标志着环境司法国际交流达到了新的高度，为今后进一步深化环境司法交流合作奠定了坚实基础，对推进国际环境法治发展，构建人与自然生命共同体具有重要意义。与会外方代表对于中国生态环境保护发展和环境司法取得的成就予以高度肯定和积极评价。联合国环境规划署官员在《世界环境司法大会中外案例汇编》序言中评价，“中国在推进环境法治方面取得了令人瞩目和振奋的成就，‘绿孔雀保护案’等典型案例的审理展示了中国环境法官积极践行环境法的各项核心原则，在全

球环境治理中处于引领地位”。

（二）提供全球环境治理司法方案

最高人民法院起草并推动通过《世界环境司法大会昆明宣言》，以传播生态文明理念、确立环境法治规则、推动构建人与自然生命共同体为目标，总结中国环境司法的原则、规则、经验和做法，达成国际环境司法“最大公约数”。《世界环境司法大会昆明宣言》明确了环境司法应秉持公平、共同但有区别的责任及各自能力原则、保护和可持续利用自然资源原则、损害担责原则“三大法治原则”，积极适用预防性司法措施、恢复性司法措施、公益诉讼和多元化纠纷解决方式“四项司法举措”，持续推动环境司法专业化、信息化、国际化“三个工作着力点”，是司法领域推动构建人与自然生命共同体的宣言，是国际环境权益保护的宣言，是国际环境司法的法治宣言，为世界各国加强全球环境危机的司法应对提供了切实可行的司法解决方案。

（三）加强环境司法案例资源共享

统筹协调国内法治和涉外法治，既关注国内环境立法、理论和实践，也打开国际视野，用案例展示这一世界各国均“听得懂的语言”，呈现中国不断演进的环境法治体系。深化与联合国环境规划署、亚洲开发银行、欧洲环保协会等国际组织合作，全面推进多领域国际司法交流，介绍中国环境资源重大典型案例，分享环境司法改革创新经验。2021 年，联合国环境规划署门户网站登载我国第二批 10 件环境资源典型案例和 2 部《中国环境资源审判》白皮书，向世界展示中国环境司法生动实践。编辑出版《中国最具影响力的十大环境案例》英文版，在巴基斯坦等共建“一带一路”国家出版发行，分享中国环境司法理念和裁判规则。

（四）参与国际研讨交流司法经验

一是“请进来”学习他国先进经验。邀请国外环境法学专家以及资深法官，就土壤污染、气候变化应对、生物多样性保护等主题，以视频方式在全国法院环境资源审判工作培训班进行交流。二是“走出去”宣传我国环境司法成就。派员参加《生物多样性公约》第十五次缔约方大会生态文明论坛、“亚太气候变化司法大会：新冠疫情时代的司法”国际研讨会、中欧应对气候变化立法研讨会、世界自然保护大会高级别圆桌会议、生物多样性保护暨预防性检察公益诉讼研讨会、中法法律与司法交流周“环境资源审判机构专业化”专题研讨会等，并作主旨发言，积极宣传中国环境司法成效。

六、展望

经过各级人民法院的共同努力，2021 年人民法院环境资源审判各项工作取得显著进展，但仍存在环境司法理念把握尚不到位、专门审判组织作用发挥不够充分、与新时代生态文明建设的要求和人民群众对优美生态环境的司法需求仍有差距等问题。下一步，各级人民法院将继续认真落实习近平主席致世界环境司法大会贺信重要指示精神，完整准确全面贯彻新发展理念，服务经济社会高质量发展，深化环境司法改革创新，持续推进审判专业化建设，巩固拓展国际交流合作，努力构建中国特色环境资源审判体系，为建设人与自然和谐共生的现代化，协同推进人民富裕、国家强盛、中国美丽提供更加有力的司法服务和保障。

附录一　2019～2021 年各级人民法院受理审结环境资源类一审案件情况

单位：件

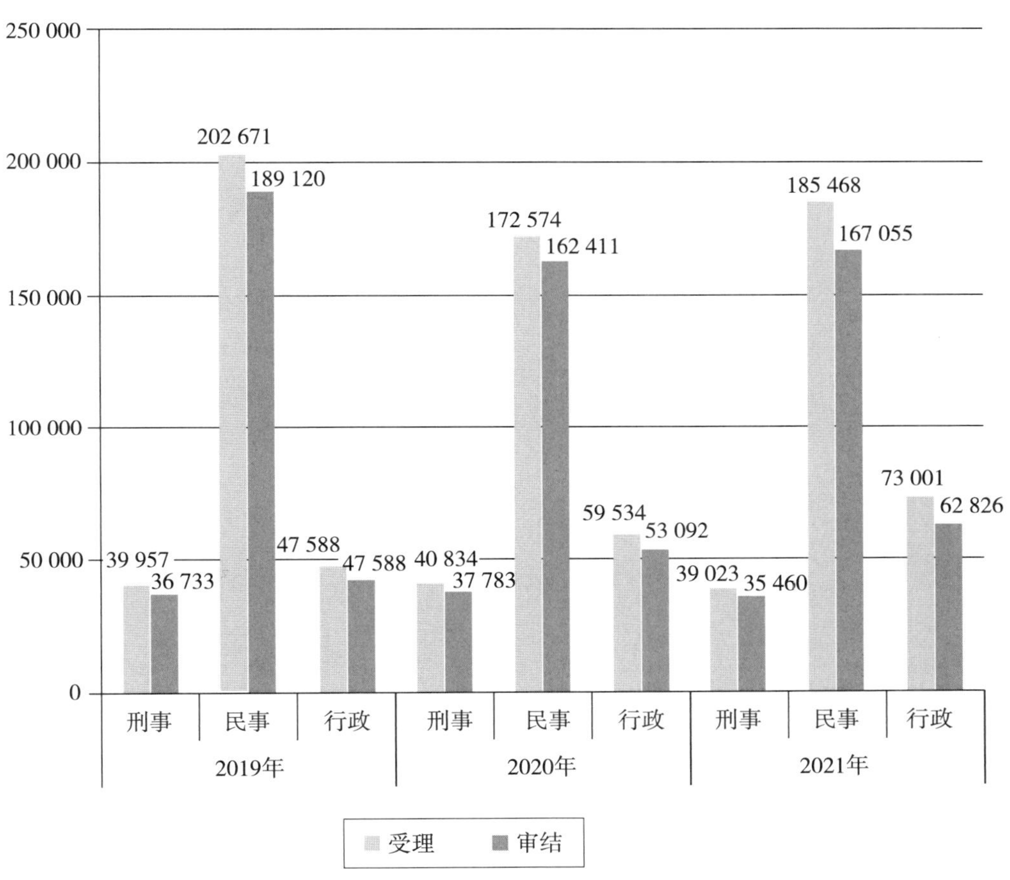

图 1　2019～2021 年各级人民法院受理审结环境资源类一审案件情况

附录二　全国法院环境资源审判机构审判组织设置情况（2021年）

表1　全国法院环境资源审判机构和审判组织设置情况汇总（共2149个）

单位：个

法院	审判庭	合议庭（团队）	人民法庭（巡回法庭）
北京	2	20	0
天津	1	6	0
河北	12	72	5
山西	16	106	11
内蒙古	11	50	3
辽宁	23	1	0
吉林	8	77	1
黑龙江	2	34	2
上海	6	13	0
江苏	19	24	9
浙江	15	72	1
安徽	75	53	8
福建	77	0	0
江西	92	26	9
山东	8	132	75
河南	12	167	7
湖北	16	114	0
湖南	21	80	6

续表

法院	审判庭	合议庭（团队）	人民法庭（巡回法庭）
广东	8	36	3
广西	8	68	8
海南	7	0	7
重庆	11	0	0
四川	119	25	41
贵州	44	0	0
云南	13	0	0
西藏	1	0	0
陕西	7	20	4
甘肃	2	19	13
青海	4	2	1
宁夏	5	5	0
新疆	2	63	1
兵团	1	0	0
军事	0	0	0
最高院	1	0	0
总计	649	1285	215

表 2　地方各级人民法院设置环境资源审判庭情况

单位：个

省份/地区	基层	中级	高级	总数
北京	1	0	1	2
天津	1	0	0	1
河北	3	8	1	12
山西	4	11	1	16
内蒙古	3	7	1	11
辽宁	16	6	1	23
吉林	5	2	1	8
黑龙江	0	1	1	2
上海	4	1	1	6
江苏	9	9	1	19
浙江	3	11	1	15
安徽	72	2	1	75
福建	66	10	1	77
江西	87	4	1	92
山东	0	7	1	8
河南	0	11	1	12
湖北	10	5	1	16
湖南	14	6	1	21
广东	3	4	1	8
广西	6	1	1	8
海南	2	4	1	7
重庆	5	5	1	11

续表

省份/地区	基层	中级	高级	总数
四川	97	21	1	119
贵州	34	9	1	44
云南	6	6	1	13
西藏	0	1	0	1
陕西	4	2	1	7
甘肃	0	1	1	2
青海	2	1	1	4
宁夏	3	1	1	5
新疆	0	1	1	2
兵团	0	0	1	1
总计	460	158	30	648

表 3　高级人民法院环境资源审判专门机构建设情况

序号	单位	机构名称	环境资源案件归口审理模式
1	北京高院	环境资源审判庭	刑事、民事、行政案件
2	河北高院	环境保护审判庭	刑事、民事、行政案件
3	山西高院	环境资源审判庭	刑事、民事、行政案件
4	内蒙古高院	环境资源审判庭	刑事、民事、行政案件
5	辽宁高院	环境资源审判庭	刑事、民事、行政案件
6	吉林高院	环境资源审判庭	刑事、民事、行政案件
7	上海高院	环境资源审判庭	刑事、民事、行政案件
8	江苏高院	环境资源审判庭	刑事、民事、行政案件
9	浙江高院	环境资源审判庭	刑事、民事、行政案件
10	福建高院	生态环境审判庭	刑事、民事、行政案件
11	江西高院	环境资源审判庭	刑事、民事、行政案件、执行（环境民事公益诉讼）案件
12	山东高院	环境资源审判庭	刑事、民事、行政案件
13	河南高院	环境资源审判庭	刑事、民事、行政案件
14	湖北高院	环境资源审判庭	刑事、民事、行政案件
15	湖南高院	环境资源审判庭	民事案件
16	广东高院	环境资源审判庭	刑事、民事、行政案件
17	广西高院	环境资源审判庭	刑事、民事、行政案件
18	海南高院	环境资源审判庭	刑事、民事、行政案件
19	重庆高院	环境资源审判庭	刑事、民事、行政案件
20	四川高院	环境资源审判庭	刑事、民事、行政案件
21	贵州高院	环境资源审判庭	刑事、民事、行政案件

续表

序号	单位	机构名称	环境资源案件归口审理模式
22	云南高院	环境保护审判庭	刑事、民事、行政、执行（环境民事公益诉讼）案件
23	陕西高院	环境资源审判庭	刑事、民事、行政案件
24	甘肃高院	环境资源保护审判庭	刑事、民事、行政案件
25	青海高院	环境资源审判庭	民事、行政案件
26	宁夏高院	环境资源审判庭	刑事、民事、行政案件
27	新疆高院	环境资源审判庭	刑事、民事、行政案件
28	安徽高院	环境资源审判庭	刑事、民事、行政案件
29	黑龙江高院	环境资源审判庭	刑事、民事、行政案件
30	新疆生产建设兵团分院	环境资源审判庭	刑事、民事、行政案件

附录三　环境资源审判相关司法解释和规范性文件（2021 年）

表 4　环境资源审判相关司法解释和规范性文件（2021 年）

	文件名称	文号	修正或发布时间	施行时间
司法解释	最高人民法院关于审理环境民事公益诉讼案件适用法律若干问题的解释（2020 年修正）	法释〔2015〕1 号	2020 年 12 月 29 日	2021 年 1 月 1 日
	最高人民法院关于审理环境侵权责任纠纷案件适用法律若干问题的解释（2020 年修正）	法释〔2015〕12 号	2020 年 12 月 29 日	2021 年 1 月 1 日
	最高人民法院关于审理矿业权纠纷案件适用法律若干问题的解释（2020 年修正）	法释〔2017〕12 号	2020 年 12 月 29 日	2021 年 1 月 1 日
	最高人民法院、最高人民检察院关于检察公益诉讼案件适用法律若干问题的解释（2020 年修正）	法释〔2018〕6 号	2020 年 12 月 29 日	2021 年 1 月 1 日
	最高人民法院关于审理生态环境损害赔偿案件的若干规定（试行）（2020 年修正）	法释〔2019〕8 号	2020 年 12 月 29 日	2021 年 1 月 1 日
	最高人民法院关于生态环境侵权案件适用禁止令保全措施的若干规定	法释〔2021〕22 号	2021 年 12 月 27 日	2022 年 1 月 1 日

续表

	文件名称	文号	修正或发布时间	施行时间
司法解释	最高人民法院关于审理生态环境侵权纠纷案件适用惩罚性赔偿的解释	法释〔2022〕1 号	2022 年 1 月 12 日	2022 年 1 月 20 日
规范性文件	环境资源案件类型与统计规范（试行）	法〔2021〕9 号	2021 年 1 月 4 日	2021 年 1 月 4 日
	最高人民法院关于新时代加强和创新环境资源审判工作为建设人与自然和谐共生的现代化提供司法服务和保障的意见	法发〔2021〕28 号	2021 年 10 月 8 日	2021 年 10 月 8 日
	最高人民法院关于贯彻《中华人民共和国长江保护法》的实施意见	法发〔2021〕8 号	2021 年 2 月 24 日	2021 年 2 月 24 日
	最高人民法院贯彻实施《长江保护法》工作推进会会议纪要	法〔2021〕304 号	2021 年 11 月 24 日	2021 年 11 月 24 日
	最高人民法院服务保障黄河流域生态保护和高质量发展工作推进会会议纪要	法〔2021〕305 号	2021 年 11 月 24 日	2021 年 11 月 24 日

附录四　最高人民法院发布环境资源指导性案例和典型案例（2021 年）

一、生物多样性保护专题指导性案例（法〔2021〕286 号，2021 年 12 月 1 日）

1. （指导案例 172 号）秦某学滥伐林木刑事附带民事公益诉讼案

2. （指导案例 173 号）北京市朝阳区自然之友环境研究所诉某水电顾问有限公司、某勘测设计研究院有限公司生态环境保护民事公益诉讼案

3. （指导案例 174 号）中国生物多样性保护与绿色发展基金会诉某流域水电开发有限公司生态环境保护民事公益诉讼案

4. （指导案例 175 号）江苏省泰州市人民检察院诉王某朋等 59 人生态破坏民事公益诉讼案

5. （指导案例 176 号）湖南省益阳市人民检察院诉夏某安等 15 人生态破坏民事公益诉讼案

6. （指导案例 177 号）海南某船务有限公司诉三沙市渔政支队行政处罚案

7. （指导案例 178 号）北海市某海洋科技有限公司诉北海市海洋与渔业局行政处罚案

二、长江流域生态环境司法保护典型案例（2021 年 2 月 25 日）

1. 被告人李某根非法捕捞水产品刑事附带民事公益诉讼案

2. 被告人赵某春等 6 人非法采矿案

3. 被告人秦某学滥伐林木刑事附带民事公益诉讼案

4. 欧某明诉重庆市铜梁区人民政府撤销行政行为案

5. 宣城市某金属铸件有限公司诉安徽省宣城市宣州区人民政府未依法履行行政补偿职责案

6. 中华环境保护基金会诉某重庆涪陵化工有限公司环境污染民事公益诉讼案

7. 北京市朝阳区自然之友环境研究所诉中国水电顾问集团某开发有限公司等环境污染责任民事公益诉讼案

8. 中国生物多样性保护与绿色发展基金会诉某流域水电开发有限公司环境民事公益诉讼案

9. 湖北省人民检察院武汉铁路运输分院诉某生态种养殖有限公司通海水域污染损害责任环境民事公益诉讼案

10. 江西省新余市渝水区人民检察院诉江西省新余市水务局怠于履行河道监管职责行政公益诉讼案

三、2020 年度人民法院环境资源典型案例（2021 年 6 月 4 日）

1. 被告人张某建等 11 人盗掘古墓葬案

2. 被告单位某保温材料有限公司、被告人祁某明污染环境案

3. 丰都县某国电站诉彭水苗族土家族自治县水利局行政处罚案

4. 湖南省益阳市人民检察院诉夏某安等 15 人非法采矿民事公益诉讼案

5. 广东省广州市人民检察院诉广州市花都区某垃圾综合处理厂、李某强固体废物污染环境民事公益诉讼案

6. 广西壮族自治区来宾市人民检察院诉佛山市某石油科技有限公司等 72 名被告环境污染民事公益诉讼案

7. 江西省上饶市人民检察院诉张某明、毛某明、张某生态破坏民事公益诉讼案

8. 江苏省南京市人民检察院诉王某林生态破坏民事公益诉讼案

9. 安徽省巢湖市人民检察院诉魏某文等 33 人非法捕捞水产品刑事附带民事公益诉讼案

10. 河南省濮阳市人民政府诉聊城某化工有限公司生态环境损害赔偿诉讼案

四、黄河流域生态环境司法保护典型案例（2021 年 11 月 25 日）

1. 刘某龙、张某君等 15 人盗伐林木案

2. 马某文非法收购、运输、出售珍贵、濒危野生动物制品案

3. 陈某强、董某师等盗掘古墓葬案

4. 买某强等6人污染环境案

5. 濮阳市人民检察院诉山东某精细化工有限公司等环境民事公益诉讼案

6. 新乡市生态环境局与封丘县某精细化工有限公司生态环境损害赔偿司法确认案

7. 济南某农场有限公司与济南市天桥区泺口街道办事处鹊山东社区居民委员会等确认合同无效纠纷案

8. 碌曲县人民检察院诉碌曲县水务水电局行政公益诉讼案

9. 某水产养殖有限公司诉三门峡市城乡一体化示范区管理委员会、灵宝市大王镇人民政府强制拆除案

10. 石嘴山市惠农区人民检察院诉石嘴山市惠农区农业农村和水务局行政公益诉讼案

Foreword

The year 2021 represented a milestone in the history of environmental resources trials for the people's courts. On May 26, President Xi Jinping noted in his congratulatory letter to the World Judicial Conference on Environment that "The Earth is our shared home. Countries must take concerted and swift actions to turn our planet into a beautiful home where humans live in harmony with nature. Guided by a new development philosophy emphasizing innovative, coordinated, green, and open development for all, China has stepped up ecological and environmental protection in all respects and taken an active part in international cooperation for ecological conservation. China has kept deepening the reform and innovation of environment-related judicial practices and has gained useful experience in protecting the ecology and environment by judicial means. China stands ready to work with other countries and international organizations to enhance global governance on environment." President Xi Jinping's congratulatory letter fully affirmed China's beneficial experience in environmental judicial reform and innovation, pointing out the direction of development and providing the people's courts with fundamental guidance in conducting environmental resources trials. On December 10, the Supreme People's Court held the Third National Conference on Environmental Resources Trials. The conference systematically summarized the past three years' work and analyzed the situation facing environmental resources trials. Besides, the conference issued specific work instructions in such areas as serving and achieving the overarching cause of building a beautiful China, striving to build a system of environmental resources trials with Chinese characteristics, actively promoting the systematization of rules for applying ecological and environmental laws, and striving to build high quality and professional judicial capability for environmental resources trials. The conference also clarified the overall thinking and future direction of judicial work, embarking on a new journey in environmental resources trials.

In 2021, courts across China adhered to the guidance of the *Xi Jinping Thought on Socialism with Chinese Characteristics for a New Era*, thoroughly implemented the *Xi Jinping Thought on Ecological Civilization* and the *Xi Jinping Thought on the Rule of Law*, as well as earnestly putting into practice the key instructions of President Xi Jinping's congratulatory letter to the World Judicial Conference on Environment. They focused on comprehensively and organically advancing the "Five-Sphere Integrated Plan" and promoting the "Four-pronged Comprehensive Strategy" in a coordinated manner, firmly followed the philosophy of people-centered development, focused on the new stage of development, built a new pattern of development and promoted high-quality development. Furthermore, courts adhered to the construction of an environmental resources trial system with Chinese characteristics as their primary task, which involved promoting the professionalization of trials as the breakthrough point, deepening reform and innovation as the driving, improving the level of "smart" justice as the support, expanding international cooperation and exchanges as the platform, so as to give full play to the functions of environmental resources trials, resulting in all work being taken to a new level.

All kinds of cases were given fair hearings in accordance with the law. In 2021, courts across China accepted 297,492 cases filed at the first instance concerning environmental resources and concluded 265,341 cases, with a year-on-year increase of 8.99% and 4.76% respectively. Courts have also intensified the punishment of crimes of environmental pollution and ecological destruction, safeguarding the country's ecological environment and natural resources. In doing so, they accepted 39,023 first-instance criminal cases and concluded 35,460 cases. Actors causing environmental pollution and ecological damage were investigated for civil liability in accordance with the law, and 185,468 first-instance civil cases concerning environmental resources have been accepted with 167,055 cases concluded. Full play has been given to the preventive and supervisory functions of administrative trials. Administrative agencies have been supported and supervised in the timely discharging of their supervisory duties in accordance with the law. In this way,73,001 first-instance cases concerning environmental and resources administration have been accepted and 62,826 cases were concluded. The trial of environmental public interest litigation and damages litigation for ecological harms has been strengthened, effectively safeguarding the interests of the country, social public interest, and the people's environmental rights and interests. In doing so, 5,917 cases of environmental public interest litigation have been accepted with 4,943 cases concluded; 169 cases of compensation for ecological damage have been accepted with 137 cases concluded.

The courts also aim to: serve and guarantee the grand mission of building a beautiful China in the new era, assist the further promotion of the nationwide battle to prevent and control pollution, implement the national strategy of biodiversity conservation, promote the efficient, economic and rational use of resources, serve low-carbon green circular development, assist in optimizing and upgrading industrial structure, serve the national strategy for regional development, and promote systematic governance in key river basins; adhere to sound law and good governance, introduce guidelines on strengthening and innovating environmental resources trials in the new era, formulate judicial interpretations and minutes of meetings such as those regarding the application of injunctions and punitive damages, publish guiding cases and typical cases, pioneer new ways of trials and enforcement, expand the adjudicatory function, and constantly improve the uniform application of judicial rules for ecological trials; continue to promote innovation and guidance, strengthen the development of specialized institutions for environmental resources trials, improve the mechanisms for specialized management, centralized jurisdiction, judicial cooperation, multi-agency coordination and alternative dispute resolution, and essentially complete a specialized environmental resources trial system; strengthen the ideological, political and professional construction of the judiciary, deepen jurisprudential research, improve judicial measures for the convenience and benefit of the people, promote judicial transparency, enhance greater public participation, and constantly improve the level of judicial services for the environmental resources; deepen international exchanges by successfully holding the World Judicial Conference on Environment, drafted and promoted the adoption of the *Kunming Declaration of the World Judicial Conference on Environment*, published typical cases and white papers of China's environmental resources on the UNEP website, and shared China's useful experience in environmental justice.

Ⅰ. Leveraging Judicial Functions to Guarantee the Overarching Cause of Building a Beautiful China in the New Era

1. Assisting in the Further Promotion of the Nationwide Battle to Prevent and Control Pollution, and the Trial of Cases on Environmental Pollution Prevention and Control in Accordance with the Law

Courts have implemented the *Opinions of the CPC Central Committee and the State Council on Fighting the Critical Battle against Pollution*, adhered to the philosophy that a sound ecological environment is of universal benefit to the people's livelihood, and made full use of judicial means to effectively safeguard the people's environmental rights and interests. People's courts at all levels have seriously cracked down on prominent illegal acts such as sewage in "secret pipes", cross-border dumping and illegal disposal of pollutants, tried cases involving air, water, soil, solid waste and noise pollution, and striven to solve prominent environmental pollution problems encountered by the people. Courts have also heard cases involving heavy urban pollution, remediation of black and odorous water, and disposal of medical waste in accordance with the law, while continuing to improve the urban living environment. In addition, they have heard cases involving agricultural diffuse pollution, soil pollution involving agricultural land and the classification of household waste in accordance with the law so as to serve the mission of building beautiful rural landscapes.

The Supreme People's Court has published typical cases involving air, water, soil, solid waste and noise pollution for further judicial guidance on pollution prevention and control. Courts have actively participated in amending the *Law on the Prevention and Control of Noise Pollution*, made suggestions on the revision of relevant provisions of legal liability, and provided practical judicial support for revising the *Law on the Prevention and Control of Noise Pollution*. Courts in the Beijing-Tianjin-Hebei region as well as the Yangtze and the Yellow River basins have intensified judicial governance of core environmental problems in their respective jurisdictions, fighting to protect the blue skies, clear waters, and clean land with ever higher standards. Local courts have strengthened the trial of cases related to medical waste disposal, which made judicial contributions to epidemic prevention and control, and maintained public health security. Courts in Shanghai have tried a civil public interest litigation case involving "foreign waste", strengthened the accountability for solid waste pollution, and generally improved the people's living environment.

In 2021, courts across the country accepted 2,837 criminal cases of environmental pollution with 2,328 concluded; 198 cases of criminal waste-smuggling cases with 167 concluded; 1,817 cases of environmental pollution disputes involving air, water, soil, solid waste and noise pollution with 1,361 concluded; 26 disputes of maritime and sea access-way pollution with 20 concluded; 17 cases of liability for ship pollution with 9 concluded; 3,377 administrative cases of environmental protection with 2,743 concluded.

2. Implementing the National Biodiversity Conservation Strategy and Trying Ecological Protection Cases in Accordance with the Law

Courts have implemented the *Opinions on Further Strengthening Biodi-*

versity Conservation issued by the General Offices of the CPC Central Committee and the State Council, systematically protected rare and endangered wild animals and plants and their living environment, and safeguarded biodiversity and biosecurity. People's courts at all levels have heard genetic diversity, species diversity, and ecosystem diversity protection related cases in accordance with the law, cracked down on all criminal activity of harming wildlife resources, punished the illegal trade in wildlife and wildlife products committed online or in other ways in accordance with the law as well as the illegal introduction, release or discarding of invasive alien species. They have strengthened judicial protection of national parks, nature reserves, and other nature parks, and protected the ecological environment of precious and endangered wildlife habitats, and the safety of migratory birds. Overall planning of the judicial protection of epidemic prevention and control, and biodiversity conservation, have been made to continuously improve China's capacity in bio-security governance.

The Supreme People's Court has issued the first batch of seven key guiding cases on biodiversity conservation, including the "green peacock protection" preemptive public interest lawsuit, and clarified rules for deciding the judicial protection of biotic populations and their living environment. Courts in the Yangtze River basin have strictly implemented the *Law of the People's Republic of China on the Protection of the Yangtze River*, promoting the restoration of aquatic biological resources in the Yangtze River by releasing judicial opinions on protection, strengthening regional judicial cooperation, and implementing a holistic crackdown on illegal fishing to promote recovery of the Yangtze River's biological resources and support the ten-year fishing ban. Chongqing courts tried the criminal case of illegally fishing for aquatic products against Li * Jian and others. The defendants were punished for their unauthorized release of invasive alien species harmful to the local ecological environment in accordance with the law, with the courts making it clear that any such proliferation and release should be in accord with the characteristics of the ecological environment to maintain local biodiversity and the waterways' ecological security.

In 2021, courts across China heard 155 cases of smuggling precious animals and animal products with 113 concluded; 3,262 cases of harming precious or endangered animals with 2,944 concluded; 177 cases of illegally hunting, purchasing, transporting and selling wild animals with 154 concluded; 3,694 cases of illegal hunting with 3,549 concluded; 5,950 cases of illegally harvesting aquatic products with 5,714 concluded; 875 cases of harming key national protected plants with 839 concluded; 1,481 cases of illegal logging with 1,407 concluded; 5,663 cases of excessive logging with 5,334 concluded; 18 cases of cronyism in the context of animal and plant bio-security with 13 concluded; 4,251 administrative cases concerning the forestry sector with 3,697 concluded; 303 administrative cases concerning the fishing sector with 281 concluded.

3. Promoting the Efficient, Economic, and Rational Use of Resources and Trying Cases of Resource Exploitation and Use in Accordance with the Law

Courts have put into practice the philosophy that "Lucid waters and lush mountains are invaluable assets", properly handled the relationship between man and nature as well as the relationship between environmental protection and development, and comprehensively promoted the efficient use of resources. People's courts at all levels have punished criminal activities which disrupt the ecological environment such as illegal mining and sand extraction, illegal occupation of rivers and lakes, excessive deforestation, destruction of trees and grass and illegal reclamation. Courts have heard cases involving the ownership of such natural resources as land, plains, mineral reserves, forests, and maritime space in accordance with the law, correctly delineated boundaries for exercising ownership and use rights of natural resources, and safeguarded the rights and interests of owners of mass-owned natural resources. They have also improved the link between administrative mediation of disputes related to the ownership of natural resources and adjudication, building a market-oriented and diversified compensation mechanism for ecological protection.

The Supreme People's Court has drafted opinions about punishing the crime of illegal mining based on the service of socioeconomic development and correctly understanding the relationship between severe punishment of crime, ecological protection, economic development, and guaranteeing the people's livelihoods. In doing so, it has given full play to the adjudicatory function of environmental resources trials, punished illegal mining according to law, effectively regulated and prevent illegal mining as well as protected the safety of mineral resources and ecological security. The Heilongjiang courts have heard a case against Wang * and others for illegal mining, seriously cracked down on illegal peat mining, and protected black soil, the "endangered species of arable land".

In 2021, courts across China have heard 4,425 cases of illegal mining with 3,549 concluded; 162 cases of purchasing and transporting illegally or wantonly felled logs with 158 concluded; 3,594 cases of illegal occupation of farmland with 3,489 concluded; 5,158 cases of disputes over use rights to construction land with 3,932 concluded; 83 cases of disputes over easements with 75 concluded; 69 cases of disputes over maritime development and exploitation with 55 concluded; 26 cases of disputes over the right to draw water with 25 concluded; 548 cases of disputes over mining rights with 423 concluded; 58,647 cases of disputes over contracts for the supply of power, water, gas and heating with 55,517 concluded; 3 cases of disputes over contracts for joint Sino-foreign exploitation of natural resources with all concluded; 11,202 cases of disputes over contracts in the farming, forestry, fishing and animal husbandry sectors with 9,874 concluded; 35,988 administrative cases related to land with 31,418 concluded; 700 administrative cases related to mining with 609 concluded; 847 administrative cases related to water conservation with 699 concluded; 17,785 other resources-related administrative cases with 15,371 concluded.

4. Serving Green, Low-Emissions Circular Development and Trying Cases of Climate Change Response in Accordance with the Law

Courts have implemented the *Working Guidance for Carbon Dioxide Peaking and Carbon Neutrality in Full and Faithful Implementation of the New Development Philosophy*, promoted synergy between pollution reduction and emission reduction, and assisted in achieving the objectives of carbon peaking and carbon neutrality. People's courts at all levels have heard cases of energy conservation and emission reduction in major emitter industries and in the development and utilization of new energy sources in accordance with the law, reducing or avoiding greenhouse gas emissions in energy, transportation, ozone-depleting substances as well as land and forestry utilization to address the global climate change crisis. Another imperative will be to accurately grasp the economic, public and ecological attributes of carbon-related rights, such as carbon credit, carbon sinks, and carbon derivatives, and properly handle relevant carbon-related civil disputes such as rights confirmation, trading, guarantee, and performance in accordance with the law. Administrative agencies will be supervised and supported in investigating and punishing illegal acts such as emitters falsifying or concealing data on greenhouse gas emissions data, and refusing to perform their obligations of reporting greenhouse gas emissions.

The Supreme People's Court has carried out thematic research on judicial rules on disputes surrounding carbon emissions trading, drafted guiding opinions to assist in achieving the objectives of carbon dioxide peaking and carbon neutrality, and issued judicial interpretations on hearing civil cases involving forestry resources. Local courts have strictly applied national laws, regulations, and policies related to pollution reduction and carbon reduction, actively explored the new characteristics of carbon-related disputes, tried carbon-related cases in accordance with the law, and jointly helped the courts achieve the objectives of carbon dioxide peaking and carbon neutrality. Maritime courts in Jiangsu, Shanghai, Zhejiang and Fujian signed a framework agreement to protect marine resources and the ecological environment in the East China Sea as well as marine "Ocean Blue Carbon" resources; Courts in Sichuan Province have established the "Green Finance Workstation for Managing Disputes at the Source" to closely follow up on issues related to the application of law involving the trading of environmental rights, such as carbon credit and energy use rights, and financing disputes; Courts in Guangdong Province have properly handled carbon emission trading contract disputes, clarifying the responsibilities of all parties; Courts in Zhejiang and Hubei Provinces issued work opinions to ensure carbon dioxide peaking and carbon neutrality.

5. Assisting in Optimizing and Upgrading Industrial Structure and Trying Cases of Ecological Governance and Service in Accordance with the Law

Courts have adopted the principle of prioritizing ecology and green development, implemented supply-side structural reform of judicial services, and promoted the comprehensive green transformation of socioeconomic development. People's courts at all levels have heard cases involving environmental impact assessments, environmental monitoring, environmental damage assessment and identification, the maintenance and operation of ecological monitoring equipment as well as facilities for pollution prevention and control, and ecological environment restoration in accordance with the law. Courts have properly heard disputes arising from the planning, construction, and production of enterprises with high energy consumption and emissions, encouraged clean production, and promoted green reform in key industries and sectors. In addition, courts have intensified efforts to handle cases involving the reform, bankruptcy, and restructuring of enterprises with high energy consumption and high emissions, and improve the market-exit mechanism. By supporting insurance companies in innovating green insurance products and services, a healthy development of the green financial market has been promoted.

Under the framework of the injunction system in civil procedure law, local courts have actively explored the application of injunctions in cases of environmental pollution and ecological damage. In doing so, they have been able to promptly prevent or reduce ecological damage, and strengthen ecological risk prevention. Courts in Fujian Province have led the way with their "Ecological Justice+Rescue Insurance" innovation and in signing cooperation agreements with insurance companies, whereby ecological restoration funds paid by the defendant go into a special company account. Courts in Jiangxi Province have explored the possibility of entrusting public welfare foundations to manage and supervise the use of ecological restoration funds and organize the implementation of environmental restoration, effectively standardizing the funds' management and use. In hearing cases of enterprises with high energy consumption and emission to restructure from bankruptcy and liquidation, courts in Zhejiang Province put forward an "environmental protection commitment" as a requirement for investment, which allows enterprises to revive through restructuring and embarking on a new development path of green and low-carbon.

6. Serving Coordinated Regional Development and Promoting the Systematic Governance of Key River Basins

Courts have implemented the principle of joint protection and coordinated governance, actively integrating ecological and judicial protection into major regional development strategies such as the development of the Yangtze River Economic Belt, construction of the Guangdong－Hong Kong－Macao Greater Bay Area, integrated development of the Yangtze River Delta, and the ecological protection and high-quality development of the Yellow River Basin. People's courts at all levels have tried environmental pollution cases involving the mainstream and important tributaries of the Yangtze River, the protection of cultural parks such as the Grand Canal and the Great Wall, and the protection of traditional dwellings, ancient villages, and historic ancient buildings so as to safeguard the environmental rights and interests of the people. Courts have heard ecological and environmental protection cases involving the Qinghai-Tibet Plateau in accordance with the law, and effectively protected the ecology of the Himalayas, subscribing to the notion that "ice-and-snow-covered lands are also invaluable assets". Courts have carefully heard cases involving the restoration and protection of key national ecological function zones as management of the source of Beijing and Tianjin's sandstorms, ecological protection and construction of Sanjiangyuan Area (the source of the three rivers, Yangtze River, Yellow River and Lancang River), ecological protection of the Qilian Mountain Range, comprehensive management of rocky desertification in karst areas. They have increased judicial protection for extremely fragile ecological areas suffering from soil, land, and coastal erosion and rocky desertification, thereby safeguarding national ecological security.

The Supreme People's Court has promulgated the *Opinions on Implementing the Yangtze River Protection Law of the People's Republic of China*, and convened progress meetings on implementing the law and on environmental resources trials for the Yellow River, Grand Canal and the South-North River Diversion Project. It has also released relevant meeting minutes and typical cases to provide guidance on adjudicatory rules for courts at all levels in serving the national regional development strategy and promoting the systematic governance of key areas and river basins in China. Local courts have deepened the centralized jurisdiction and judicial collaboration of environmental resources cases in key regions. Courts in Anhui, Jiangxi, Hubei and Hunan Provinces have signed the *Framework Agreement on Judicial Coordination Relating to Environmental Resources of the Middle and Lower Reaches of the Yangtze River*, reaching a consensus on strengthening cross-regional environmental judicial cooperation in the area; Hebei has organized eight primary courts along the Grand Canal to sign the *Memorandum of Understanding on Coordinating Judicial Protection of Ecological Resources for the Grand Canal*(*Cangzhou Section*) and implemented integrated protection. Courts in Beijing have heard the "Great Wall Protection Case", aiming at strengthening historical and cultural heritage protection.

Ⅱ. Adhering to Sound Law and Good Governance, Constantly Improving the System of Rules for Environmental Resources Trials

1. Further Promoting the Top-Level Design of Judicial Policy

The Supreme People's Court has held the Third National Work Conference for Environmental Resources Trials, systematically summarizing work results, deeply analyzing the situation at hand, putting forward the construction of a trial system with Chinese characteristics and international reputation as a key work priority, and clarifying the overall objective of providing strong judicial support for modernizing the construction of harmonious coexistence between man and nature as well as coordinating the promotion of the prosperity of the people, national strength and a beautiful China. With a view to serving the overall construction of a beautiful China, deepening reform and innovation, promoting the systematic application of laws and rules as well as building a high-quality and professional judiciary, the Supreme People's Court has planned environmental resources trials in a scientific manner and made specific work arrangements. The *Opinions on Strengthening and Innovating Environmental Resources Trials in the New Era to Provide Judicial Services and Guarantees for Modernizing the Harmonious Coexistence between Man and Nature* issued by the Supreme People's Court puts forward comprehensive guidance and specific requirements for the people's courts in all fields and stages of environmental resources trials in the new era. The *Rules for Categorizing and Enumerating Environmental and Resource Cases (for Trial Implementation)* guides courts at all levels to reasonably delimit the scope of environmental resources cases and the scope of responsibilities of courts or tribunals for environmental resources trials, ensuring that such trials do not stray from their main responsibilities. Courts in Heilongjiang, Jilin, Guizhou and Qinghai Provinces have issued normative rules in light of their respective jurisdiction's characteristics to promote the high-quality development of environmental resources trials.

2. Improving the Rules for the Application of Laws

The Supreme People's Court has issued the *Provisions on the Application of Injunctions in Ecological Tort Cases*, implementing the principle of prioritizing protection and prevention, promptly and effectively protecting the ecological environment as well as safeguarding the legitimate rights and interests of civil subjects. It has also issued the *Interpretation on the Application of Punitive Damages in Environmental Tort Cases* to enforce the strictest possible ecological protection under the rule of law, intensify judicial sanctions against malicious ecological damage and strike a balance for environmental trials between ecological protection, socioeconomic development and ensuring people's livelihood. The formulation and promulgation of these two judicial interpretations have played a leapfrog role in ecological protection, and the two judicial interpretations have been widely welcomed by the courts at all levels and fully endorsed by relevant administrative agencies and academic communities. The system of rules has been constantly improved through the drafting of judicial interpretations on civil disputes involving forest resources, rules of evidence for civil litigation in environmental torts, and the participation of persons with technical knowledge as people's assessors in environmental resources cases. The High Courts in Hainan and Chongqing issued sentencing guidelines, the Guizhou High Court issued trial guidelines and the Shandong and Henan High Courts issued case management regulations and other documents to further strengthen the trial of environmental resources cases.

3. Giving Full Play to the Exemplary Effect and Supplementary Authority of Cases

The Supreme People's Court has strengthened the guidance of environmental resources cases; improved the working mechanism for the discovery, cultivation, and recommendation of guiding cases; improved the pertinence, rationality, and operability of case compilation and selection; and clarified the criteria for application of laws. The first seven guiding cases concerning biodiversity protection were released in 2021, and the selection of the second batch of guiding cases concerning environmental public interest litigation has been started. Efforts have been made to give full play to the exemplary effect of typical cases, enhance the researches on the application of laws to difficult, complicated, and novel cases, and promote the uniformity of the judgment rules in different types of cases concerning environmental resources. The year 2021 witnessed the publication of a total of 30 typical cases including cases concerning ecological and environmental protection of the Yangtze River and the Yellow River and typical cases of 2020, and the mediated settlement or retrial of *All-China Environment Federation (ACEF) v. Guoneng Liaoning * Environmental Protection Industry Group Co., Ltd.* and other civil public interest lawsuits concerning environmental pollution, for the purpose of promoting the timely and effective ecological and environmental restoration. According to the requirements for the reform of the trial-level functional positioning of the courts at four levels, efforts have been made to constantly improve the mechanism for granting certiorari over environmental resources cases of new types, with universal guidance for the application of laws and with significant controversies over application of laws, the problem of insufficient adjudication rules has been resolved. Sichuan court's trial of the public interest lawsuit concerning the protection of Acer pentaphyllum can guide the intensified preventive judicial protection of precious and endangered wild plants. Jiangxi court's trial of the public interest lawsuit concerning environmental pollution caused by illegal dumping of chemical waste liquids constituted a useful exploration for the correct application of the punitive damages clause on ecological and environmental infringement in the *Civil Code*.

4. Innovating the Way of Conducting Trials and Expanding Adjudicatory Functions

Courts have been committed to restorative justice and innovated and applied a variety of restoration methods that meet the ecological and environmental protection requirements in view of the restoration needs with different environmental factors. In the trial of the civil public interest lawsuit concerning air pollution by an automobile manufacturing company, Shandong court explored "green enforcement", urging the defendant enterprise to realize ecological restoration by donating electric vehicles for public welfare undertakings, and coordinating economic development and environmental protection as a whole. Jiangxi court explored the charitable trust mechanism of entrusting an ecological and environmental foundation to monitor the restoration funds in public interest lawsuits and coordinate the implementation of ecological and environmental restoration with positive results. The courts in Fujian, Zhejiang, Sichuan and Guizhou Provinces have ordered the tortfeasors to fulfill their legal liability for ecological and environmental restoration by subscribing to carbon credit in court proceedings or enforcement, promoting pollution control and carbon reduction. The courts in Xinjiang and Ningxia Provinces have established a mechanism for return visits in enforcement to ensure that the obligation of ecological and environmental restoration will be effectively fulfilled.

The requirements for restorative justice have been implemented, and innovative adjudication methods have been explored. In criminal cases, defendants' proactive restoration of ecology and environment, afforestation, proliferation, setting free animals and other acts in line with the laws of nature are considered attenuating factors of lighter sentencing, so as to promote the timely restoration of the damaged ecology and environment. In civil cases, the concerned business' funds for continued technological upgrading and transformation while having already met the national environmental standards will be deducted for technological transformation to offset the ecological and environmental restoration expenses, so as to promote the business' green transformation and upgrading. The purpose is to give full play to the role of ecological and environmental restoration bases and carry out diversified ecological protection, publicity, restoration, and other work. Courts in Hubei set up 44 protection bases in key areas; Courts in Gansu carried out the restoration bases, having cumulatively achieved the regreening area of 8,600 *mu* (≈ 573.3 hectares), more than 150,000 replanted plants, and an average annual carbon dioxide neutralization capacity of about 9,886 tons.

Ⅲ. Continually Guiding Innovation and Striving to Build an Environmental Resources Trial System with Chinese Characteristics

1. The basic formation of a system of environmental resources trials

As of the end of 2021, there had been 2,149 specialized courts and tribunals for cases concerning environmental resources in China, consisting of 649 trial courts for environmental resources (including the Supreme People's Court, 29 high people's courts, Xinjiang Production and Construction Corps Branch of Xinjiang High People's Court, 158 intermediate people's courts, and 460 primary people's courts), 215 people's tribunals, and 1,285 trial teams (collegiate bench). Following the establishment of Nanjing and Lanzhou Environmental Resources Courts, the Supreme People's Court approved the establishment of Kunming and Zhengzhou Environmental Resources Courts, exploring new practices in specialized judicial bodies. Courts across China set up circuit courts, environmental protection courts, tourism courts, etc. in key basins, world natural heritage sites, river sources, national parks, nature reserves, etc. , to strengthen the judicial protection of key ecological function areas. All 16 prefecture-level cities in Shandong Province set up environmental resources trial courts, and 155 primary courts identified 187 environmental resources trial institutions; Guizhou sets up 114 judge workstations for judicial protection of traditional villages.

2. Widespread implementation of a system of centralized trial and jurisdiction

In 2021, the Supreme People's Court centralized the criminal, civil, and administrative trial functions for environmental resources to the environmental resources trial division, and further improved the supervision of and guidance for lower courts. A total of 27 high people's courts and Xinjiang Production and Construction Corps Branch of Xinjiang Higher People's Court adopted the "three-in-one" centralized trial mode for criminal, civil, and administrative cases concerning environmental resources, among which The High People's Courts in Jiangxi, Yunnan and other Provinces adopted the "four-in-one" centralized trial and enforcement mode for criminal, civil, administrative and enforcement cases.

The diversified mode of centralized jurisdiction across administrative divisions was improved. Kunming Environmental Resources Court has centralized jurisdiction over the first instance, second instance and retrial of environmental resources-related cases previously heard by the intermediate courts in Yunnan Province. Zhengzhou Environmental Resources Court has centralized jurisdiction over the cases concerning environmental resources along the trunk stream of Huaihe River and the South-to-North Water Diversion Project. Hubei courts initially formed a "1+5+10+N" specialized system for trial of environmental resources-related cases, which was composed of the high court, the intermediate courts, the ecological and environment protection tribunals, and the trial teams. Hainan High People's Court, the procuratorial office, and the Coast Guard jointly signed the opinions on the pilot work of centralized designated jurisdiction over specific maritime criminal cases, centrally designating the maritime courts to have jurisdiction over two types of cases, namely, crimes of maritime traffic accidents, and crimes of destroying marine ecological and environmental resources. Zhejiang Province has adjusted the mode of jurisdiction over the cases concerning environmental resources in Huzhou to "South Taihu Lake Court's centralized jurisdiction over the entire administrative region plus the designated jurisdiction over Anji and other key areas". Sichuan Province has set up the Giant Panda National Park Ecological Court, which is responsible for centralized jurisdiction over related cases in the Sichuan part of the Giant Panda National Park, realizing the integrated judicial protection of regional environmental resources.

3. Maturity of judicial cooperation mechanism construction

All local courts have implemented the principle of integrated protection and systematic governance and continuously deepened judicial cooperation in environmental resources in view of the characteristics of key regions and basins. The Supreme People's Court held a meeting to promote the trial of cases concerning environmental resources in the basins of the Yellow River, the Grand Canal, and the South-to-North Water Diversion Project, further strengthening the judicial protection and cooperation in ecological, environmental and cultural resources in the basins of the Yellow River, the Grand Canal and the South-to-North Water Diversion Project. The High People's Courts in Henan, Hubei and Shaanxi signed the agreement on cooperation in ecological and environmental protection and restoration of Danjiangkou Reservoir; The High People's Courts in Heilongjiang and Inner Mongolia signed the agreement on cooperation in the trial of cases concerning the protection of forests, grasslands, wetlands and wildlife resources in the two provinces (regions) in the northeast frontier; Courts in Henan and Beijing courts signed the agreement on cooperation in the development of a judicial demonstration base for water conservation under the rule of law in the starting and ending areas of the Middle Route of the South-to-North Water Diversion Project; The High People's Courts in Hubei, Hunan and Jiangxi Provinces signed a cooperation mechanism for trial work in the urban agglomeration in the middle reaches of the Yangtze River; The High People's Courts in Tianjin, Liaoning and Shandong signed the agreement on judicial cooperation in ecological and environmental protection of Bohai Sea; seven intermediate people's courts and maritime courts along the East China Sea in Zhejiang Province established the "1+7" mechanism for judicial cooperation around the East China Sea, constantly strengthening judicial cooperation in key regions and basins.

4. Constant expansion in the inter-agency joint action mechanism building

The Supreme People's Court signed a collaborative governance agreement with the Office of the Leading Group for Promoting Ecological Protection and High-quality Development of the Yellow River Basin, and held a discussion with the Ministry of Ecology and Environment, promoting the coordination and linkage between administrative law enforcement and judicial work. China's courts, ecological and environmental administrations, and other authorities jointly issued opinions on administrative law enforcement and judicial cooperation mechanism for ecological, environmental, and resource protection, so as to address the difficulty in cooperation among regions in judicial and administrative protection. Courts, ecological and environmental administrations and other authorities of Jiangsu, Shanghai and Zhejiang signed the minutes of the meeting on the mechanism for the mutual recognition of ecological and environmental inspection and law enforcement in the Yangtze River Delta Integration Demonstration Zone; Guangxi High People's Court and the administrations signed the framework agreement on cooperation in ecological and environmental protection in Lijiang River Basin and Beibu Gulf; Shaanxi High People's Court, procuratorial authorities and other authorities signed the measures for linkage between administrative law enforcement and criminal justice in forestry; the courts and procuratorial authorities of Liaoning and Tianjin, among others, signed the opinions on the trial of cases concerning environmental public interest litigation and other aspects; Hainan High People's Court and procuratorial authorities jointly issued the sentencing guidance on standardized sentencing in cases concerning illegal logging and deforestation commonly seen in the tropical rain forest national park, facilitating the construction of Hainan Tropical Rainforest National Park.

5. Effectiveness of alternative dispute resolution mechanism building

Courts all over China promoted the use of alternative dispute resolution methods such as mediation, consultation, and arbitration to more efficiently and conveniently meet people's diverse judicial needs concerning environmental issues. To give full play to the positive role of judicial advice, Courts in Guangdong Province put forward judicial advice on working with an Internet company in deleting more than 30,000 illegal online posts, intercepting 175 groups of keywords related to wildlife, and providing criminal clues for public security authorities when handling wildlife-related criminal cases. Efforts were made to carry forward the "Fengqiao Experience" in the new era, give play to the role of people's courts and circuit trials in grassroots-level environmental governance, and create models of grassroots-level environmental justice in conflict resolution. On its own initiative, the People's Court of Simao District, Pu'er Municipality, Yunnan Province extended its judicial functions, setting up China's first "Legal Service Station for Human-Elephant Harmony" in the domicile of the "Asian Elephant Breeding Center", which strengthened the source prevention and front-end resolution of human-elephant conflicts and disputes, promoted the resolution of human-elephant conflicts and disputes into the green channel of rule of law, and explored a new mode of litigation source governance and environmental resources cases trial. Courts in Fujian Province explored the integration of the forest chief system and justice, and established a network for resolving forest-related ecological disputes before litigation based on the key aspects of forest-related ecological governance.

Ⅳ. Strengthening team building and improving environmental justice

1. Deepening theoretical studies and improving professional expertise

The interaction of judicial practice and theory has been enhanced due to the efforts being made to bring into play the role of the Environment and Resources Judicial Research Center of the Supreme People's Court. Particularly, in terms of environment-related provisions of the *Civil Code*, researches on practical issues such as legal applications, selection of papers and special symposiums have been designed to promote the integrated development of theory and practice. In 2021, theoretical research centers and practice centers released a total of 24 research findings of various types. That year also witnessed the launch of an online training course on trials of environmental and resource cases for courts across China by the Superme Peoples's Court; a training workshop was held in cooperation with the China Environmental Protection Foundation for judges in the central and western regions of China on environmental and resources trials; a "Green Development Forum" was held with Chinese and international experts, scholars and senior judges invited for exchanges and trips to Zhejiang, Shaanxi, Yunnan and other Provinces in China to conduct intensive research on environmental and resource adjudication; a nation-wide selection of excellent judgment documents and outcomes in environmental and resources trials was organized. In the selection, 15 judgment documents from courts in Yunnan, Chongqing, Jiangsu and other Provinces, as well as research results submitted by 19 courts in Beijing, Zhejiang, Guangdong and other Provinces were awarded, which has effectively improved the expertise of personnel in the judicial system. To meet requirements for specialized trials of environmental and resource cases, local courts across China have strengthened training and conducted special research to enhance the professional capabilities of judges and clerks.

2. Sweeping away obstacles to litigation and further improving judicial measures to provide the public with greater convenience

By fully implementing one-stop diversified dispute resolution and litigation services, and improving judicial measures, the Supreme People's Court has provided great convenience and benefits to people, and continues to increase the scale of high-quality environmental justice. Active efforts are being made to promote the development of smart courts and accelerate the establishment of China's judicial platform for environment and resources. Online case filing, cross-jurisdiction case filing, online court hearings, and circuit court trials have enabled the parties involved to conveniently participate in litigation. Courts in Chongqing have set up a circuit court for judicial cooperation on environmental and resource cases to provide people in Sichuan Province and Chongqing Municipality with efficient and easily accessible cross-jurisdiction litigation services featured by all-in-one integration of case filing, trial, and enforcement; a court in Jiangsu Province has set up a "Circuit Court Station for the Judicial Protection of the Ancient Grand Canal" for community circuit court trials; courts in Xinjiang have adopted a circuit court mode of "being stationary and mobile" and assigned judicial officers to circuit court trial stations to provide "door-to-door" judicial services; a court in Shandong Province has used a boat for circuit court trials in the Weishan

Lake Basin, making judicial services highly accessible to the people.

3. Promoting judicial openness and reinforcing public participation

The people's courts at all levels have rigorously implemented the open trial system by broadcasting trials live through various types of media platforms such as the China Court Trial Online, WeChat official accounts, Weibo, etc. For environmental and resource cases that have a significant impact on the jurisdiction, the people's courts have proactively invited deputies to people's congresses, members of the National Committee of the Chinese People's Political Consultative Conference (CPPCC), representatives of relevant enterprises and the public as well as students to be present in courtrooms for the trials, with a view to enhancing the openness and transparency of trials. In 2021, the Supreme People's Court held 6 special press conferences to issue judicial interpretations, guiding cases, etc.; 85 deputies to the National People's Congress and members of the CPPCC National Committee were invited to participate virtually in the third national conference on trials of cases on environment and resources and other major events. Publicity about environmental justice has been strengthened through the WeChat official account of "Environmental and Resource Adjudication in China". The Supreme People's Court guided the people's courts at all levels to hold press conferences to release annual reports and typical cases, and to conduct public hearings and other publicity activities on landmark dates such as June 5th (World Environment Day), so as to form an intensive demonstration effect and effectively extend the influence of environmental justice. For lawsuits, mediation agreements, restoration plans, or any other matters involving environmental civil public interest litigation cases and ecological and environmental damages cases, the announcement procedure is strictly implemented, so as to put the judicial process under public supervision, protect the people's rights to know, participate in and supervise environmental justice.

V. Deepening international exchanges and sharing the experience and best practices in China's environmental justice

1. The World Judicial Conference on Environment

In May 2021, in advance of the 15th Conference of Parties to the *UN Convention on Biological Diversity* in Kunming, the Supreme People's Court of the People's Republic of China and the United Nations Environment Programme (UNEP) jointly organized the World Judicial Conference on Environment with the theme of "Role of the Judiciary in Advancing Ecological Civilization: Building a Shared Future for All Life on Earth." President Xi Jinping sent a congratulatory letter to the Conference, fully affirming the beneficial experience of China in the reform and innovation of environmental justice. In his letter, President Xi also charted the course in strengthening international exchanges and cooperation in environmental justice and promoting the global environmental rule of law. Mr. Zhou Qiang, President and Chief Justice of the Supreme People's Court, delivered a keynote speech, fully showing vivid examples of judicial protection of the ecology and environment in China. Over 160 Chinese and international delegates attended the Conference. They were Chief Justices, Justices, Presidents, and Judges of supreme courts, constitutional courts and supreme administrative courts from 27 countries including

Russia and French, representatives of international organizations like the UNEP, foreign diplomats, as well as Presidents of 8 high people's courts of Yunnan and other provinces of China. The attendees had in-depth exchanges and discussions on the role of the judiciary in global environmental governance, adjudication principles of environmental cases, judicial protection of biodiversity, and judicial response to climate change. Moreover, the *Kunming Declaration of the World Judicial Conference on Environment* was unanimously adopted at the Conference. The success of the World Judicial Conference on Environment has consolidated the international consensus on the judicial protection of the global ecology and environment, signifying that the international exchanges on environmental justice have reached a new height. It not only laid a solid foundation for further deepening the exchanges and cooperation in environmental justice in the future but also had great significance in building a community of life between humans and nature. At the Conference, international representatives spoke highly of China's achievements in the development of ecological and environmental protection and environmental justice. A UNEP official commented in the preface to the *Case Report of the World Judicial Conference on Environment* that "China had made remarkable and exciting achievements in promoting the environmental rule of law, and that the handling of typical cases such as 'the green peafowls' habitat protection case' demonstrated judges for environmental cases in China had been actively practicing the core principles of environmental protection law, leading the global environmental governance".

2. Providing judicial solutions for global environmental governance

The Supreme People's Court drafted and facilitated the adoption of the *Kunming Declaration of the World Judicial Conference on Environment*, with the goal of communicating the philosophy of ecological civilization, establishing the principle of upholding the rule of environmental law, and building a community of life for mankind and nature. By sharing the principles, rules, experiences, and practices of China's environmental justice, the Supreme People's Court aims to find the "largest common ground" for global environmental justice. As specified in the *Kunming Declaration of the World Judicial Conference on Environment*, the three principles of the rule of law should be observed in environmental justice, namely, the principle of equity, common but differentiated responsibilities and respective capabilities, the principle of protection and sustainable use of natural resources, as well as the "polluter pays" principle. The use of four judicial measures should be advocated, i. e., to actively adopt preventive judicial measures, to preferentially apply restorative judicial measures, to explore and improve the public interest litigation system, and to encourage the use of diversified dispute resolution methods. Moreover, continuous efforts should be made to promote the professional, information technology-based, and international development of environmental justice. The *Kunming Declaration of the World Judicial Conference on Environment* reveals the judiciary's resolution to facilitate the building of a community of life for mankind and nature. It is a declaration on the protection of environmental rights and interests worldwide, and on the rule of law in international environmental justice. Thanks to the declaration, countries around the world can access practical and feasible judicial solutions to strengthen judicial responses to global environmental crises.

3. Strengthening resource sharing in the adjudication of environmental cases

The overall coordination of the rule of law in China and international legal practice has been enhanced. While focusing on environmental legislation, theoretical study, and practices in China, courts in China have been fostering a global perspective. By using case sharing as a "universal language" that all countries in the world can understand, the courts have presented the evolving environmental rule of law system in China. Cooperation with international organizations such as the UNEP, the Asian Development Bank, and ClientEarth is being enhanced to comprehensively promote international judicial exchanges in various fields. In this respect, courts in China would like to introduce domestic major typical cases on environment and resources, in addition to sharing innovative experiences in environmental judicial reform. In 2021, the UNEP posted ten typical environmental and resource cases in China (second batch) and two white papers titled *Environmental and Resources Adjudication in China* on its website, showing the practice of China's environmental justice to the world. The English version of *Top* 10 *Influential Environmental Cases in China* has been published in Pakistan and other countries participating in the Belt and Road Initiative to share the philosophy and principles of China in environmental justice and adjudication rules.

4. Participating in international seminars to exchange judicial experience

Best practices in other countries have been "brought in". International experts on environmental law and senior judges were invited to the Training Program for Courts in China on the Adjudication of Environmental and Resource Cases. They exchanged views on topics such as soil pollution, response to climate change, biodiversity protection, etc. through a video conferencing system. "Going global" to highlight the achievements of China's environmental justice, representatives were sent to participate in many international conferences and delivered keynote speeches. For instance, the Ecological Civilization Forum of the 15th Conference of Parties to the *UN Convention on Biological Diversity*, the Asia-Pacific Judicial Conference on Climate Change: Justice in the Era of COVID-19, the China-EU Workshop on Climate Change Legislation, the World Conservation Congress High-level Roundtable, Symposium on Biodiversity Conservation and Preventive Prosecution Public Interest Litigation, and Symposium on the Specialization of Judicial Authorities for the Adjudication of Environmental and Resource Cases of the Sino-French Legal and Judicial Exchange Week. Through these conferences, courts in China have actively communicated the effectiveness of domestic environmental justice.

Ⅵ. Looking into the Future

Through the joint efforts of the people's courts at all levels, significant progress has been made in trials of environmental and resource cases in 2021; however, there are still challenges to be addressed, for example, the insufficient understanding of the principles of environmental justice, underplayed role of specialized judicial organs, and the gap between the requirements for ecological progress in the new era and the people's judicial needs for a pleasant and well-protected environment and ecology. Moving forward, the people's courts at all levels will continue to put into practice the spirit of the instructions given by President Xi Jinping in his congratulatory letter to the World Judicial Conference on Environment, and it is required for courts to fully and faithfully implement the new development philosophy on all fronts to facilitate high-quality economic and social development. In addition, the reform and innovation of environmental justice will be deepened, with continuous efforts to promote judicial specialization. People's courts will also cement and extend international exchanges and cooperation, striving to build a judicial system for the environment and resources with Chinese characteristics. All the endeavors aim to provide more solid judicial services and guarantee for the harmonious coexistence between mankind and nature, and for coordinated promotion of the prosperity of the people and nation as well as the beauty of China's landscape.

Annex 1 First-Instance Environmental and Resource Cases Accepted and Concluded by People's Courts at All Levels (2019-2021)

Unit:Piece

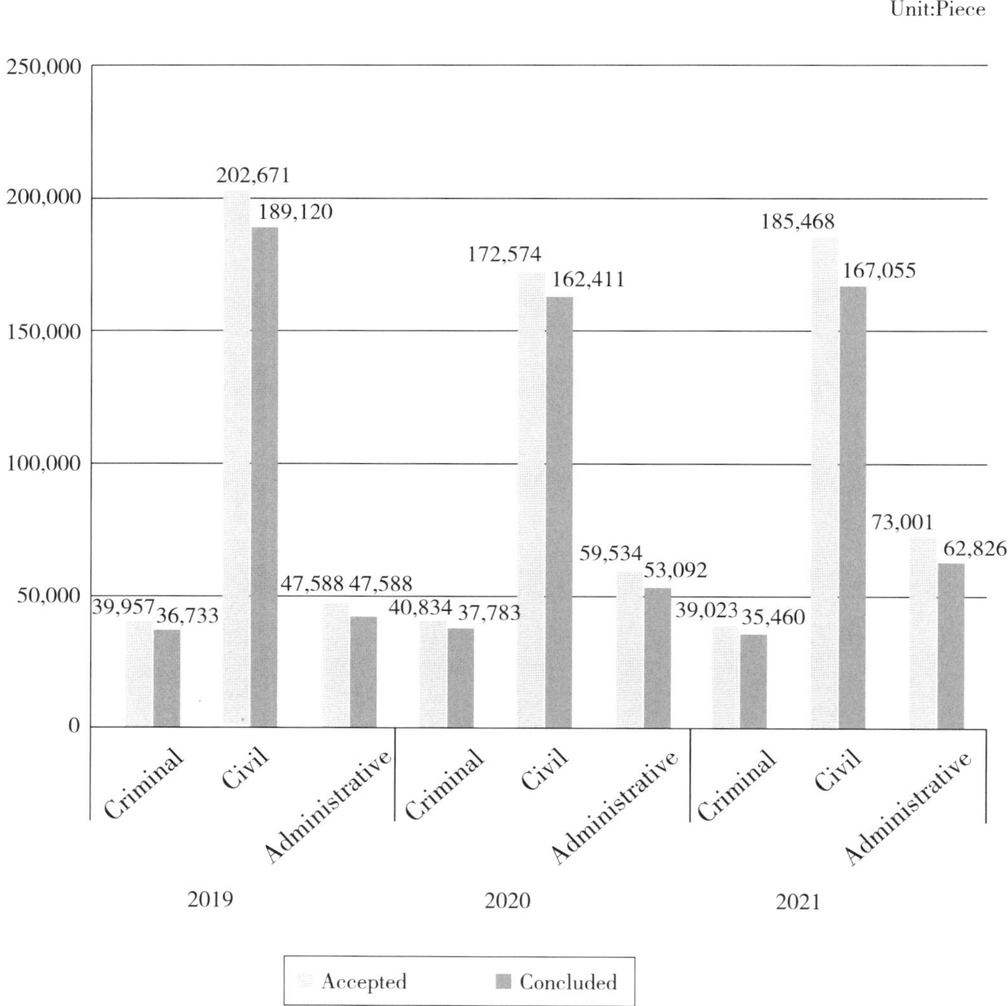

Figure 1 First-Instance Environmental and Resource Cases Accepted and Concluded by People's Courts at All Levels (2019-2021)

Annex 2 Setup of Environment and Resources Divisions/ Tribunals Across China

Table 1 Setup of Environment and Resources Divisions/ Tribunals Across China(2,149 in total)

Unit: Benches

Courts	Divisions	Collegial Benches (Team)	Dispatched People's Tribunals (Circuit Courts)
Beijing	2	20	0
Tianjin	1	6	0
Hebei	12	72	5
Shanxi	16	106	11
Inner Mongolia	11	50	3
Liaoning	23	1	0
Jilin	8	77	1
Heilongjiang	2	34	2
Shanghai	6	13	0
Jiangsu	19	24	9
Zhejiang	15	72	1
Anhui	75	53	8
Fujian	77	0	0
Jiangxi	92	26	9
Shandong	8	132	75
Henan	12	167	7

(Continued)

Courts	Divisions	Collegial Benches (Team)	Dispatched People's Tribunals (Circuit Courts)
Hubei	16	114	0
Hunan	21	80	6
Guangdong	8	36	3
Guangxi	8	68	8
Hainan	7	0	7
Chongqing	11	0	0
Sichuan	119	25	41
Guizhou	44	0	0
Yunnan	13	0	0
Xizang	1	0	0
Shaanxi	7	20	4
Gansu	2	19	13
Qinghai	4	2	1
Ningxia	5	5	0
Xinjiang	2	63	1
Production and Construction Corps	1	0	0
Military Court	0	0	0
The Supreme People's Court	1	0	0
Total	649	1,285	215

Table 2 Setup of Environment and Resources Divisions by People's Courts at All Levels

Unit: Benches

Province/Region	Primary People's Court	Intermediate People's Court	High People's Court	Total
Beijing	1	0	1	2
Tianjin	1	0	0	1
Hebei	3	8	1	12
Shanxi	4	11	1	16
Inner Mongolia	3	7	1	11
Liaoning	16	6	1	23
Jilin	5	2	1	8
Heilongjiang	0	1	1	2
Shanghai	4	1	1	6
Jiangsu	9	9	1	19
Zhejiang	3	11	1	15
Anhui	72	2	1	75
Fujian	66	10	1	77
Jiangxi	87	4	1	92
Shandong	0	7	1	8
Henan	0	11	1	12
Hubei	10	5	1	16
Hunan	14	6	1	21
Guangdong	3	4	1	8

(Continued)

Province/Region	Primary People's Court	Intermediate People's Court	High People's Court	Total
Guangxi	6	1	1	8
Hainan	2	4	1	7
Chongqing	5	5	1	11
Sichuan	97	21	1	119
Guizhou	34	9	1	44
Yunnan	6	6	1	13
Xizang	0	1	0	1
Shaanxi	4	2	1	7
Gansu	0	1	1	2
Qinghai	2	1	1	4
Ningxia	3	1	1	5
Xinjiang	0	1	1	2
Production and Construction Corps	0	0	1	1
Total	460	158	30	648

Table 3 Setup of Environment and Resources Divisions by the High People's Courts

Unit: Benches

No.	Court	Organ	Centralized adjudication of environmental and resource cases
1	Beijing High People's Court	Environment and Resources Division	criminal, civil and administrative cases
2	Hebei High People's Court	Environmental Protection Division	criminal, civil and administrative cases
3	Shanxi High People's Court	Environment and Resources Division	criminal, civil and administrative cases
4	Inner Mongolia High People's Court	Environment and Resources Division	criminal, civil and administrative cases
5	Liaoning High People's Court	Environment and Resources Division	criminal, civil and administrative cases
6	Jilin High People's Court	Environment and Resources Division	criminal, civil and administrative cases
7	Shanghai High People's Court	Environment and Resources Division	criminal, civil and administrative cases
8	Jiangsu High People's Court	Environment and Resources Division	criminal, civil and administrative cases
9	Zhejiang High People's Court	Environment and Resources Division	criminal, civil and administrative cases
10	Fujian High People's Court	Ecology and Environment Division	criminal, civil and administrative cases

(Continued)

No.	Court	Organ	Centralized adjudication of environmental and resource cases
11	Jiangxi High People's Court	Environment and Resources Division	criminal, civil, administrative and enforcement (environmental civil public interest litigation) cases
12	Shandong High People's Court	Environment and Resources Division	criminal, civil and administrative cases
13	Henan High People's Court	Environment and Resources Division	criminal, civil and administrative cases
14	Hubei High People's Court	Environment and Resources Division	criminal, civil and administrative cases
15	Hunan High People's Court	Environment and Resources Division	civil cases
16	Guangdong High People's Court	Environment and Resources Division	criminal, civil and administrative cases
17	Guangxi High People's Court	Environment and Resources Division	criminal, civil and administrative cases
18	Hainan High People's Court	Environment and Resources Division	criminal, civil and administrative cases
19	Chongqing High People's Court	Environment and Resources Division	criminal, civil and administrative cases

(Continued)

No.	Court	Organ	Centralized adjudication of environmental and resource cases
20	Sichuan High People's Court	Environment and Resources Division	criminal, civil and administrative cases
21	Guizhou High People's Court	Environment and Resources Division	criminal, civil and administrative cases
22	Yunnan High People's Court	Environmental Protection Division	criminal, civil, administrative and enforcement (environmental civil public interest litigation) cases
23	Shaanxi High People's Court	Environment and Resources Division	criminal, civil and administrative cases
24	Gansu High People's Court	Environmental and Resource Protection Division	criminal, civil and administrative cases
25	Qinghai High People's Court	Environment and Resources Division	civil and administrative cases
26	Ningxia High People's Court	Environment and Resources Division	criminal, civil and administrative cases
27	Xinjiang High People's Court	Environment and Resources Division	criminal, civil and administrative cases
28	Anhui High People's Court	Environment and Resources Division	criminal, civil and administrative cases

(Continued)

No.	Court	Organ	Centralized adjudication of environmental and resource cases
29	Heilongjiang High People's Court	Environment and Resources Division	criminal, civil and administrative cases
30	Xinjiang Production and Construction Corps Branch High People's Court	Environment and Resources Division	criminal, civil and administrative cases

Annex 3 Judicial Interpretations and Normative Documents Related to Environmental and Resource Adjudication(2021)

Table 4 Judicial Interpretations and Normative Documents Related to Environmental and Resource Adjudication(2021)

	Document	Document No.	Date of Amendment or Release	Effective Date
Judicial Interpretations	Interpretation of the Supreme People's Court on Several Issues Concerning the Application of Law in the Trial of Cases Involving Environmental Civil Public Interest Litigations (Amended in 2020)	Judicial Interpretation [2015] No. 1	December 23, 2020	January 1, 2021
	Interpretation of the Supreme People's Court of Several Issues Concerning the Application of Law in the Trial of Cases Involving Disputes over Liability for Environmental Torts (Amended in 2020)	Judicial Interpretation [2015] No. 12	December 23, 2020	January 1, 2021
	Interpretation of the Supreme People's Court on Several Issues Concerning the Application of Law in the Trial of Cases Involving Disputes over Mining Rights (Amended in 2020)	Judicial Interpretation [2017] No. 12	December 23, 2020	January 1, 2021

(Continued)

	Document	Document No.	Date of Amendment or Release	Effective Date
Judicial Interpretations	Interpretation of the Supreme People's Court and the Supreme People's Procuratorate on Several Issues Concerning the Application of Law in Cases Involving Procurate-filed Public Interest Litigation (Amended in 2020)	Judicial Interpretation [2018] No. 6	December 23, 2020 December 28, 2020 (the Supreme People's Procuratorate)	January 1, 2021
	Provisions of the Supreme People's Court on Handling Cases of Ecological Damage Compensation (Trial) (Amended in 2020)	Judicial Interpretation [2019] No. 8	December 23, 2020	January 1, 2021
	Provisions of the Supreme People's Court on the Application of Injunction and Preservation Measures in Cases Involving Environmental Torts	Judicial Interpretation [2021] No. 22	December 27, 2021	January 1, 2022
	Interpretation of the Supreme People's Court on the Application of Punitive Damages in the Trial of Cases Involving Disputes Over Environmental Torts	Judicial Interpretation [2022] No. 1	January 12, 2022	January 20, 2022

(Continued)

	Document	Document No.	Date of Amendment or Release	Effective Date
Normative Documents	Types of Environmental and Resource Cases and Statistical Specifications (Trial)	Fa [2021] No. 9	January 4, 2021	January 4, 2021
	Opinions on Strengthening and Innovating Environmental and Resource Adjudication in the New Era and Providing Judicial Services and Guarantees for the Harmonious Coexistence Between Humans and Nature	Fafa [2021] No. 28	October 8, 2021	October 8, 2021
	Opinions on Implementing the *Yangtze River Protection Law of the People's Republic of China*	Fafa [2021] No. 8	February 24, 2021	February 24, 2021
	Minutes of the Coordination Meeting of the Supreme People's Court on Implementing the *Yangtze River Protection Law of the People's Republic of China*	Fa [2021] No. 304	November 24, 2021	November 24, 2021

(Continued)

	Document	Document No.	Date of Amendment or Release	Effective Date
Normative Documents	Minutes of the Coordination Meeting of the Supreme People's Court on Providing Judicial Services for the Ecological Protection and High-quality Development in the Yellow River Basin	Fa [2021] No. 305	November 24, 2021	November 24, 2021

Annex 4 Catalogue of Guiding Cases and Typical Cases on Environment and Resources Issued by the Supreme People's Court(2021)

Ⅰ. Guiding Cases on Biodiversity Conservation (Fa [2021] No. 286, December 1, 2021)

1. (Guiding Case No. 172) People v. Qin * xue on indiscriminate deforestation, a criminal collateral civil public interest litigation case

2. (Guiding Case No. 173) Friends of Nature Environmental Research Institute, Chaoyang District, Beijing v. HydroX Corporation and * Engineering Corporation Limited, a civil public interest litigation case on ecological and environmental protection

3. (Guiding Case No. 174) China Biodiversity Conservation and Green Development Foundation v. Yalong Hydro Co., Ltd., a civil public interest litigation case on ecological and environmental protection

4. (Guiding Case No. 175) The People's Procuratorate of Taizhou City, Jiangsu Province v. 59 persons including Wang * peng, a civil public interest litigation case over liability for ecological damage

5. (Guiding Case No. 176) The People's Procuratorate of Yiyang City, Hunan Province v. 15 persons including Xia * an, a civil public interest litigation case over liability for ecological damage

6. (Guiding Case No. 177) Hainan * Shipping Co., Ltd. v. Sansha Municipal Fishery Administration Detachment, an administrative penalty case

7. (Guiding Case No. 178) Beihai * Marine Technology Co., Ltd. v. Beihai Ocean and Fishery Bureau, an administrative penalty case

Ⅱ. Typical Cases Concerning the Judicial Protection of the Ecology and Environment in the Yangtze River Basin (February 25, 2021)

1. People v. Li * gen for illegal fishing of aquatic products, a criminal collateral civil public interest litigation case

2. People v. the accused Zhao * chun and other 5 persons for illegal mining

3. People v. Qin * xue for indiscriminate deforestation, a criminal collateral civil public interest litigation case

4. Ou * ming v. the People's Government of Tongliang District of Chongqing Municipality on revocation of an administrative act

5. * Metal Casting Co., Ltd. in Xuancheng City v. the People's Government of Xuanzhou District, Xuancheng City, Anhui Province for failure in performing statutory administrative compensation duties

6. China Environmental Protection Foundation v. Sinochem Fuling Chongqing Chemical Industry Co., Ltd., a civil public interest litigation case over liability for environmental pollution

7. Friends of Nature Environmental Research Institute, Chaoyang District, Beijing v. Hydrochina Corporation * Development Co., Ltd. et al., a civil public interest litigation case over liability for environmental pollution

8. China Biodiversity Conservation and Green Development Foundation v. Yalong Hydro Co., Ltd., an environmental civil public interest litigation case

9. Wuhan Railway Transportation Branch of the People's Procuratorate of Hubei v. * Ecological Farming Co., Ltd., an environmental civil public interest litigation case on liability for ecological damage caused by pollution of waters leading to the sea

10. The People's Procuratorate of Yushui District, Xinyu City, Jiangxi Province v. Xinyu Water Authority, Jiangxi Province, an administrative public interest litigation case for neglecting to perform the duties of river course supervision

Ⅲ. Typical Cases Concerning Environment and Resources in 2020 (June 4, 2021)

1. People v. the accused Zhang * Jian and other 10 persons for ancient tomb robbing

2. People v. the defendant entity * Thermal Insulation Material Co., Ltd. and the defendant Qi * ming on liability for environmental pollution

3. * State Grid Station in Fengdu County v. Water Conservancy Bureau of Pengshui Miao and Tujia Autonomous County, an administrative penalty case

4. The People's Procuratorate of Yiyang City, Hunan Province v. 15 persons including Xia * an for illegal mining, a civil public interest litigation case

5. The People's Procuratorate of Guangzhou City, Guangdong Province v. * Garbage Treatment Plant in Huadu District, Guangzhou City and Li * qiang, a civil public interest litigation case concerning environmental pollution by solid waste

6. The People's Procuratorate of Laibin City, Guangxi Zhuang Autonomous Region v. 72 defendants including Foshan * Petroleum Technology Co., Ltd., a civil public interest litigation case on liability for environmental pollution

7. The People's Procuratorate of Shangrao City, Jiangxi Province v. Zhang * ming, Mao * ming and Zhang *, a civil public interest litigation case on liability for ecological damage

8. The People's Procuratorate of Nanjing City, Jiangsu Province v. Wang * lin, a civil public interest litigation case on liability for ecological damage

9. The People's Procuratorate of Chaohu City, Anhui Province v. 33 persons including Wei * wen for illegal fishing of aquatic products, a criminal collateral civil public interest litigation case

10. The People's Government of Puyang City, Henan Province v. * Chemical Co., Ltd. in Liaocheng, an ecological and environmental damages case

Ⅳ. Typical Cases Concerning the Judicial Protection of the Ecology and Environment in the Yellow River Basin(November 25, 2021)

1. People v. 15 persons including Liu * long and Zhang * jun for illegal logging

2. People v. Ma * wen for illegal acquisition, transportation and sale of

products of precious and endangered wildlife

3. People v. Chen * qiang and Dong * shi and others for ancient tomb robbing

4. People v. 6 persons including Mai * qiang for environmental pollution

5. The People's Procuratorate of Puyang City v. Shandong * Fine Chemical Co. ,Ltd. et al. ,an environmental civil public interest litigation case

6. Case of declaratory judgement confirming the compensation for ecological and environmental damage between Xinxiang City Ecological Environment Bureau and Longrun Fine Chemical Co. ,Ltd. of Fengqiu County

7. Jinan * Farm Co. ,Ltd. v. Queshan Dong Neighborhood Committee of Luokou Sub-district Administration Office, Tianqiao District, Jinan City, a dispute over contract invalidity

8. The People's Procuratorate of Luqu County v. Water and Hydropower Authority of Luqu County, an administrative public interest litigation case

9. * Aquaculture Co. , Ltd. v. the Urban-Rural Integration Demonstration Zone Administrative Committee of Sanmenxia City and the People's Government of Dawang Town of Lingbao City for their forced demolition of facilities

10. The People's Procuratorate of Huinong District, Shizuishan City v. the Agriculture, Rural Affairs and Water Authority of Huinong District, Shizuishan City, an administrative public interest litigation case